May 6 1992

To Mollie Lee
with love
M

Mollie Lee Lyon

ISH KABIBBLE

# ISH KABIBBLE

The Autobiography of

MERWYN BOGUE

With Gladys Bogue Reilly

Louisiana State University Press
Baton Rouge and London

Manufactured in the United States of America
98 97 96 95 94 93 92 91 90 89 5 4 3 2 1

Designer: Sylvia Malik Loftin
Typeface: Palatino
Typesetter: G&S Typesetters, Inc.
Printer: Thomson-Shore, Inc.
Binder: John H. Dekker & Sons, Inc.

Library of Congress Cataloging-in-Publication Data

Bogue, Merwyn, 1908–
Ish Kabibble : the autobiography of Merwyn Bogue / with Gladys Bogue Reilly.
p. cm.
Includes index.
ISBN 0-8071-1498-7 (alk. paper)
1. Bogue, Merwyn, 1908– . 2. Jazz musicians—United States–Biography. 3. Entertainers—United States—Biography. I. Reilly, Gladys Bogue, 1900– II. Title.
ML419.B635A3 1989
788'.1'0924—dc19
[B] 88-29213
CIP



Unless otherwise noted, all illustrations are from the Bogue family collection.

The paper in this book meets the guidelines for permanence and durability of the Committee on Production Guidelines for Book Longevity of the Council on Library Resources. ♾

To Janet Meade Bogue
My bride and joy

and in memory of
Kay Kyser
My Big Band boss for twenty years
and
Gladys Bogue Reilly
Without whom this book would not have been possible

If you tell the truth,
you don't have to remember
anything.

—*Mark Twain*

# Contents

# Illustrations

# 1

## BOYHOOD AND YOUTH
## THE DAYS PRIOR TO ISH

## Peanuts and Pool

Man, when you gotta ask what it is, you'll never get to know.

—Louis Armstrong, on being asked to define New Orleans jazz

Before I was out of high school, I was Big Band crazy. When Paul Whiteman brought his band to Erie for a week at the Perry Theater on 10th Street, I went to their first show alone. Like the teenager who wants to suffer alone or ride Cloud Nine alone, I wanted to listen to Paul's great music all by myself.

I found a front row seat in the center and fidgeted on the edge of it for what seemed an interminable time, waiting for the curtain to go up. It finally rose to a long drum roll, and there stood Paul himself. He and his band were all in white, shining uniforms, and as he led his band, he looked right down at me. Then he introduced his brand new act.

Out to center stage sailed a miniature organ on a little platform on wheels. Leaning way out from it were Bing Crosby and Harry Barris, clutching the organ with one hand and waving to the audience with the other, while Al Rinker's hands danced over the organ keys. The audience went wild. To cheering and roaring applause, the three belted out their recorded hit, "Mississippi Mud," and the crowd hurrahed.

The band did four shows a day that week, and I saw every one. There was a two-hour movie, then the stage show. The performers had those two movie hours to kill somewhere. I never saw the movie. After the first stage show, I made a dash for the outside stage door, hoping to see the boys up close and maybe get some autographs.

But when they appeared, they never looked my way, and I

turned chicken. They started down the street. I followed a few feet behind. When I realized where they were going—to a second-floor speakeasy on State Street—I decided to go with them. I had never been in a speakeasy, so I wondered, as I climbed the stairs behind them, whether I would be allowed in.

The boys muttered a password through the little peephole. A door opened, and we all went inside. The owner must have considered me part of the group. But nobody knew me from Eephus, and I sat off in a corner by myself. The three of them got something to drink, scooped handfuls of peanuts from a big glass penny machine, and sat telling stories. I was so afraid they would be late for their next show that I appointed myself their timekeeper. I decided that if they got too interested in their stories and their time was getting short, I would say, "Hey, fellows, you better start walking back or you'll miss your next show." When I finally said it, they looked at me as though to say, "Who are you?" But they got up and left. After this had happened a few more times, one of them said, "Thanks, kid." They were never late for a show that whole week, and I was sure that it was because of my timekeeping.

The next time I saw Bing Crosby in person was almost twenty years later. In 1949 I got a call from Frank Capra to be in a movie with Bing called *Ridin' High* at Paramount. I sang one entire song to Bing face to face. The name of the song was "The Owner Told the Trainer, the Trainer Told the Jockey, the Jockey Told the Horse, and the Horse Told Me." I asked Bing one day between takes if he remembered a kid in an Erie speakeasy who always got him to the theater on time. He did a double take, swung his golf club at another wad of Kleenex, and said: "Well, I'll be . . . . Was that *you*? Hey, those were the greatest peanuts I ever ate!"

In Erie the Whiteman Band stayed at the Lawrence Hotel at Tenth and Peach. At 10th and Sassafras, one block west, the cathedral's chimes rang out every hour, playing a few notes and then tolling the hour—one, two, three—and you could hear it all over downtown Erie. The first four notes went like this:

The first four notes of the Erie chimes were in Gershwin's *Rhapsody in Blue*! Where had Gershwin gotten them? Had Whiteman told Gershwin about the Erie chimes? Perhaps the phrase haunted Whiteman or Ferde Grofé, one of Paul's arrangers at that time. Was Grofé in Erie with Paul?

A year or so later I learned that Whiteman had commissioned Gershwin to write a jazz piece for a Whiteman concert in New York's Aeolian Hall to be held in February, 1924, and *Rhapsody in Blue* was the result. Recently I read Charles Schwartz's *Gershwin: His Life and Music,* which suggests that Grofé had a lot to do with the writing of the *Rhapsody.* In fact, Paul Whiteman asked Grofé to orchestrate the piece as fast as Gershwin wrote it. But for several years I thought that the source of the famous first four notes of *Rhapsody in Blue* was the Erie cathedral's chimes. I suppose I *wanted* to believe that, since Erie was practically my hometown. Then I learned that other cathedrals in other cities the world over had been playing those same notes for a hundred years or more. So the famous phrase was not Erie's, at least not exclusively. No wonder, though, that whenever I heard *Rhapsody in Blue,* chills ran up and down my spine. I felt very close to those notes, having heard them every day since I could remember anything.

I could hardly believe Gershwin had written such great music at the age of twenty-five. What would *I* be doing at age twenty-five? I felt uneasy, wishing I were older and doing something to talk about. I fumbled for my handkerchief and blew my teenaged nose.

That Whiteman week made my whole world open up. I grew up; it was an awakening. I was another person, fired with a new enthusiasm for my cornet lessons and a desire to be part of something big that I could not yet define. Suddenly I was aware that I lived in the U.S.A.—not just in Erie. And Erie had grown in stature for me; on the national show-business map it was more important than I had thought. Big musicians booked Erie.

One more year of high school blocked my view of the future. I was vaguely aware that I was expected to go to college to study law. Why, I was not sure. The family thought I should. It was something one did. It was "the plan" for me. But when I daydreamed, my fingers beat time to some familiar song or a bit of new melody. I never had daydreams of myself as a lawyer pleading a case.

Almost every day after school I would go down to the basement of the Lawrence Hotel with Jerry Thompson, and we would shoot pool. Jerry played tuba. We went there to meet other Erie musicians who were always stopping in. When I first began to go, I had bouts with my conscience. For I had been told a story that nagged at me every time I picked up a cue stick to play a game of pool.

About 1910, when I was two or three years old, before my mother got sick, Billy Sunday came to Erie to hold revival meetings. A huge tabernacle was erected for him. It held hundreds of folding chairs and had sawdust on the floor. He was in Erie for six weeks. At each service every chair was taken, and people stood at the sides and in the back. My mother attended often, sometimes taking my two older sisters, Marie and Gladys.

Billy Sunday was a famous revivalist, and he always put on a good show. People went as much to see his lively performance as to hear his words. Both his body and his soul went into his sermons. Screaming praise to the Lord and damnation to the Devil, he literally threw himself back and forth across the platform. He would leap onto a rickety folding chair he kept on the stage and, with hands raised high toward heaven, thunder out his message. He made people laugh, and he made them cry. He wound up every session physically exhausted—no voice left, wringing wet. He would plead and plead, hoarsely, until the people poured down the aisles to kneel at his feet and be "converted," in some cases no doubt for the umpteenth time. Whatever else one might think about Billy Sunday, it was certainly true that by the time he left town, it seemed he had washed a multitude of Erie souls. No one who watched him could ever forget him.

My mother thought he was great, though she wished her girls did not have to listen to all his "swear words"—his talks were peppered with them. It seemed to her that he should be able to preach without such expressions. But apparently he could not. He had too large a collection of them, I suppose.

About this time the YMCA of Erie installed pool tables in its recreation area. My mother, now that she had me, a boy, was worried. She had been strictly brought up by an English father,

Shem Parsons, who frowned on such goings-on as card playing, dancing, Sunday newspaper reading, and similar evils, and who, furthermore, lived at a slight angle across the street and was thus able to watch every social move my mother made. So, worried about her boy and the threat of the pool tables, in an incident much like one in *The Music Man,* my mother wrote a letter to Billy Sunday requesting his candid opinion of a Christian association that would encourage the young men of Erie to play pool. Would this not lead them to other undesirable activities? she asked him. She received a prompt reply that I have today somewhere in my files: "I can't say I approve, but perhaps it will keep the young men off the streets," the famed revivalist said.

That is the story that nagged me whenever I picked up a cue stick in the basement of the Lawrence Hotel. At first I always wondered if I should silently apologize to my mother. But then I always said to her, under my breath, "But if you had lived, you would have changed your ideas by now, wouldn't you?" For some time I worked at talking myself into believing in this change of attitude on her part, until finally I could pick up a cue stick with her everlasting blessing.

## The White Dove

"Where did you ever get the name Ish Kabibble?" is what people I meet always ask me—almost every day, in tones of disbelief. The real question they seem to be asking is why anyone would choose to be called such a thing.

Choose it? I didn't. Audiences of the Kay Kyser Band *put* that name on me. Customers at the Blackhawk Restaurant in Chicago danced past our bandstand and yelled over the music: "Hey, you with the trumpet, Ish Kabibble! Do your song!" They gave *me* the name of the song. I've been stuck with it ever since.

Obviously, I was not born Ish Kabibble. I swear it. My folks never even considered the name. At first they called me simply "the boy." I was the family's first boy, following a whole caboodle of sisters and girl cousins. After a few names were tossed around, my mother pulled a boy's name out of her sleeve. She had seen the name somewhere and liked it. I have often wondered if she picked it up from the Merwin Manufacturing Company in Erie. Wherever she got it, my sisters tell me she wanted it spelled with a *y*. So Merwyn with a *y* I am.

It was a cold day when I was born. I know that, because it was January—January 19, 1908, in the town of North East, on the shores of cold Lake Erie. Not that North East has ever openly claimed me. It does proudly claim Kay Williams, as it should. Any town would if it could.

Kay and I once had a conversation about our common birthplace. Mrs. Clark Gable and Ish Kabibble from the same place? Unlikely, but true.

For weeks after I was born, all I had to do was lie there and swing my arms or snooze. Nothing to worry about. Me worry? "No, not me!" says the Ish Kabibble song.

Then one spring morning—so I have been told—North East went into a near panic. Colorful wagons of gypsies had been spotted a mile away, heading toward the town. Frantic families gathered children, grabbed wash off clotheslines, pulled shades, locked doors, hid. Soon gypsies covered the town, street by street. They meant business. They banged on our front door, got no answer, and went around to the back, walking fast, stopping only long enough to pick a choice apple from one of our trees. Clothing of many colors was their trademark, with headkerchiefs tied at the back.

"Come on! Open up!" they called out, snapping their fingers for emphasis. They wanted food and clothing—the whole town knew that from other years. But what else might they take? People were afraid to open the door and afraid not to.

Storekeepers downtown worried. If they did not give, the gypsies took, stacking armfuls of groceries, yard goods, hardware, and whatever else took their fancy, into their boldly decorated wagons, which followed them down the street. A fast ransacking of a helpless town. Of course, North East had a jail. One cell!

Several days later, rumor had it that the gypsies had broken camp outside town and moved on. Our hired girl took me for a ride, so the story goes, in my baby carriage. She got as far as a neighborhood grocery, a block away, when she saw three gypsies taking long strides in her direction. Scared out of her skull, she ran home, leaving me behind. The gypsies stopped to look me over. The grocer saw them through his window and ran out to rescue me, taking me inside for safe keeping. It was widely believed that gypsies sometimes kidnapped small babies.

That same year my folks moved the family back to Erie after only two years in North East. Owning and running a lumber mill was out of my father's system; he was hungry to build again. Martin Henry Bogue, contractor and builder, was a self-made man, a joker, and a good-looker. He never got past the fourth grade in school, because his father had needed all his sons on his Kimball Hill farm near Union City, Pennsylvania. It was no ordinary need, but a desperate one. My grandfather—James Hubbard Bogue—lost all his savings of three thousand dollars three times in three different bank failures in the days before bank deposits were insured. He also lost his wife. If he had anything to leave to his eleven children, it was grit and guts and honesty.

As Dad put it once, when times got rough in the Great Depression, "I say let the whole world go to hell and we'll all start over." He often said, "All anybody has to do is get to goin' it."

When Dad built a new house for us across the street, he put everything into it that my mother wanted: dumb waiter, fruit cellar, clothes chute, broom closet, spice cupboard, marble-slab worktables, and walls of oak cupboards from floor to ceiling. I was four when we moved, and the whole process was burned into my memory. Of course, I could carry only small things. At first we moved things directly across the street. It was a dirt road. On rainy days my two sisters and I were allowed to go barefoot in the road puddles and let the cool mud ooze between our toes.

Right in the middle of the move, the city started to pave East 21st Street. Streets were not paved in a day. So we had to carry everything down to Wayne Street, cross 21st Street on wooden planks, and struggle down the other side of the street to our new number, 817.

Everyone was excited. We were going to have heat in our bedrooms and electric lights all through the house. All we had to do, Dad said, was flick a switch, whatever that was, and there would be light. There would be no more gas mantles that crumbled or blew away like the white fluff of a dandelion if you as much as touched them and no more waiting in the semi-darkness for someone to strike a match, keep it lighted, and adjust the gas jet, one room at a time.

My own small bedroom was close to the top of the stairs. The wallpaper, which was chosen just for me, had a border near the ceiling with a row of big animals—elephants, tigers, lions. Those animals were about eighteen inches high, and when the moonlight flickered through my window, I could not get to sleep, because the animals seemed to come alive and walk. Scared, I would call to my father downstairs, "Give de boy a dink of water."

Time after time Dad would come upstairs, patiently get me a glass of water, and say good night once more. He was the one who mostly took care of me, because my mother was sick a lot. He could have told me to get my own drink, but he knew that I was scared and that it was upsetting my mother. I heard them talking one night: "And we thought he would love that paper!" But finally, I would call one time too many. Dad would yell up the stairs, "Aw, dry up with ya!"

I did not know how sick my mother was. But we had not been in the new house long before she was in bed all the time. Dad carried steaming hot towels upstairs for some pain at the back of her neck. He could never get them hot enough for her unless he heated them in the oven downstairs. Sometimes, if my two sisters were not home, Dad sent me to the corner drugstore for medicine. Mr. Russell, the druggist, would say, "Hold it tight, Merwyn." I would run home with it as fast as I could, so that it could make Mama better.

I remember some of these events; others I was only told. But I clearly remember that I sat on my mother's bed a lot, to be near her. One day my Aunt Flora, Dad's sister, came, and I did not want her there; I did not want anybody there but me. She brought a sweater she said she had knitted for me, and she tried to give it to me while I was sitting on Mama's bed. I told her I did not like it. A handmade sweater was not what I wanted. All I wanted was for Aunt Flora to go away and leave us alone.

I was four when my mother died that summer, two months after we moved into the new house. I have no recollection of anyone telling me of her death, though I do remember the day Dad came down to Aunt Min's, a few houses away, where, for some reason unknown to me, I had been staying for a few days. He dressed me in some new clothes, and we walked down to our house. He held my hand tight, and his voice did not sound right. He told me that a lot of people were at our house, that I should sit at the top of the stairs, and that he would see me later and we would talk.

A girl cousin sat with me on the top steps. She said I was too little to be downstairs. But I could hear churchy talk and nose blowing. What was the matter? Our front room was full of people, some of whom I had never seen before. From where we sat, I could not see the front room, so I kept sliding down a step or two to peek. But my cousin's hand kept hold of my shirt, and every time I tried to ask a question, I was shushed. I wanted to know where my mother was. I knew she was away. At Aunt Min's I had heard talk about Mama being "gone." Well, when would she be back?

I kept trying to peek. All I wanted was to get a good look at a stuffed white dove that seemed to be flying over a lot of flowers in our front room. I never had time to get a good look. I would get only a brief glimpse of the bird, and then that hand would yank me back.

My most vivid memory of the days that followed my mother's death is climbing the stairs to the attic whenever I thought I was alone in the house and getting a big picture of my mother that Dad had put up there for his own reasons. I would take the picture down to my room. It was heavy and almost as big as I was. I would sit on my bed and look at Mama and whisper things and cry. I would kiss her face and beg her to come back. When someone slammed the back door downstairs, I rushed the picture back to the attic as quietly as I could.

Our attic was always a special place for me, since, in a way, she was up there. It was nice and warm, too, and smelled of Dad's freshly cut wood.

## Jelly Bread Days

In she come,
Down she sot,
She laid an egg,
And up she got.
—Ish

One housekeeper after another tried to suit us; for various reasons none of them did. Then my father telephoned a woman who had worked for us in North East—a motherly type. She could come. But of course she would have to live in.

One night after supper I heard her talking in low tones to Dad in the kitchen. Suddenly Dad's voice rose: "I'll give you exactly ten seconds to get your stuff in the car!" What it was all about is anybody's guess. Dad never told me the good part—what she had said. But any number of times I have watched him enjoy telling what he did next: "I drove her that fifteen miles to North East in nothing flat. She spent most of the time in the air, her head bumping the top. I hit every bump in the road I could see, driving like blazes, headed for Kingdom Come! She must have thought I'd gone crazy. She sure was glad to get out of that car!" And he would laugh and laugh.

After that, Dad would not have a housekeeper in the house. He sent my sister Marie, who was fourteen, away to school; Gladys, twelve, went to stay with Aunt Flora, two blocks away. I went to Aunt Min's, five houses down the street. He slept at home.

Every afternoon about 5:30, I stood in front of Aunt Min's and watched for Dad's car to turn into our driveway. Then I ran down to see him and we talked.

My Grandfather Parsons, my mother's father, lived at Aunt Min's, too. Or was it that Aunt Min lived with him? I never knew. Grandpa's back had been broken years before and was never set, so he walked bent over. That was fairly common in those days—I had other older relatives with unset broken backs.

He and I spent hours on his porch swing. He had rigged up a contraption to cut pears off one of his trees without ever moving from the swing. He had a long pole with a razor blade attached to the end somehow. Under the razor blade was a large tin can with no top. A string ran from the razor blade all the way down the pole so that he could stay in his seat while he got a pear in just the right position over the can. Then he pulled the string that moved the blade that cut the stem. The pear would drop into the can. That was one pear. Then he did it again. Two pears. That was all we needed, the two of us. We would laugh, Shem Parsons and I.

A couple of years went by. One day my father told me that a new lady was coming into our house and he was going to marry her. I did not like the idea. I had seen her in church, but how could she be my mother? The night came when there was to be a party at our house and I would meet her. Lots of people were coming. By now I was seven, and so I ran away to a friend's house at Twenty-sixth and Wayne. I stayed until I thought the party was over; then I went home. As soon as I saw Dad, I saw trouble. He grabbed my collar and marched me to the barn and whipped me with a switch he pulled from a backyard bush.

But he must have loved me, too, for shortly after that I asked him for a real live pony from the pony track at Waldameer Park. He took me into the living room and showed me the mantelpiece. "When the top of your head touches the bottom of this mantelpiece, I'll get you a pony," he said. "By then you'll be old enough. We'll go out to Waldameer Park, and you can pick one out."

Every night after dinner I would stand under that mantel. I thought I would never make it. But one night I realized I was almost there, and in a short time I did make it.

He and I had often been out to the pony track at Waldameer, and I had had lots of rides on a pony named Bird. That was the pony I wanted and that was the one I got. To get the pony home, we tied him to the back of our car and pulled him slowly along. But he did not want to go. After a few yards, he spread his two front feet and balked. We had to coax him for two hours before we got him home. I would ride Bird around the neighborhood. Dad got me a pony cart, and we would sometimes deliver small lumber supplies to some house that he was building.

One day, just for fun, we entered him in a competition at the racetrack out at the fairgrounds. It was not a formal competition, but the ponies had to follow directions, circling around barrels and such. Bird and I were ready. But something scared him, and he bolted, jumped over a rail and threw me, and made for the exhibit where jams and jellies and pies were on display. Helter-skelter went the jars and pumpkin pies. It was not funny until afterward.

Whenever there was a county fair going on, Dad and I were there the first day. A small side attraction at one fair was run by a man who had a mongoose and a monkey; he advertised that they would soon fight to the death. The mongoose was caged, but the monkey was fastened by a long chain to a stake in the ground. People made a big fuss over the monkey, and I fed him peanuts all day. I did not get too close, just throwing the peanuts in his direction. The owner did not like my doing this, and one morning the monkey made his usual leap toward me, but this time he got me, biting me in the fat part of my hand below the thumb. I still have the scar today. The owner had lengthened the chain or moved the stake without my realizing it. The owner never did come through with the "fight to the death."

Recently I saw a television interview with Carl Sandburg's daughter. She said her father had "walked her on the ceiling" when she was a child. I could hardly believe it for I had thought that walking on the ceiling was something only I, in the whole world, had experienced. Arriving home from work, Dad would pick me up and turn me over upside down till my feet touched the ceiling, and say, "Walk!" I have always liked Carl Sandburg's poems, but now I feel a rapport with his daughter.

When I got older—sometimes when I was home from college—he would pick me up and walk me on the ceiling. I weighed 160 pounds by then. After I had married Janet, we went home for dinner one night, and he picked me up. Embarrassed, I started to resist, for I was a big boy now. But it was no use—he was strong. So I walked on the ceiling in front of Janet, with Dad and me both laughing so hard we could hardly do it. That was in 1932, and Dad was sixty years old. He was incredible.

When I was eight, before my pony days, I started taking piano lessons. For a wedding present Dad had bought Mabel, his new wife, a grand piano, and he wanted me to learn something about music because he never had. Every evening he would ask Mabel to play. She was good, since she had studied at Oberlin and taught music in Oak Park schools in Chicago. They found a teacher for me, but my heart was not in piano.

Also about this time, I decided I wanted a cherry tree. I pestered Dad for one. "If George Washington could have one, why can't I?" I asked. Soon he brought one home and planted it. One day I chopped it down with my ax. When Dad got home that night, he asked me who did it. I said, "I did, but you can't whip me, 'cause I told the truth." He whipped me.

Although we lived right in the middle of town, our barn was really a barn. In it Dad kept his two horses, two lumber wagons, a Hudson car, an old Maxwell, my pony and cart, and occasionally a cow that he would fatten up for winter food. Upstairs in the barn was the hay to feed and bed down the horses. On the alley side of the barn was a double door through which hay was pitched into the hayloft. It was up in that hayloft that I organized all the neighborhood kids into my club.

It was my backyard, my barn, and my club. Everybody could have a say, but I was in charge. That meant that I got to decide what you had to do to be a member, which was to jump out our second-story hayloft door, down into the alley, without breaking a leg. When I told the kids that, they all stared at me. Some wise guy thought it only fair that I go first. I was ready. I had been practicing. Was that cheating? I could not have those kids doubt that I was worthy of being their leader.

On initiation day I jumped and landed all right. Bob Cooney jumped and made it. Next, Dan Bryner made it. Then Mortzy, from down the block, jumped and broke his leg. So we had to kick him out of the club.

By the time he could almost walk again, we had reorganized. From the heights we had switched to the depths. I formed a club to dig down into the ground to China. I asked Dad to build me a small clubhouse in the backyard, which he did. I told him I wanted to raise rabbits. That was not a lie; we did raise rabbits for a while. But secretly we kids met each day inside the clubhouse and dug a little more. The clubhouse hid the hole; we did not want the whole world to know our plans. Surely my father knew what was going on. He was not one to walk around with his eyes shut. But he never said a word, so I figured he just did not care if we were digging a hole to China.

We dug for several days, and the hole was getting rather deep. We continued our work, though by this time only three of us could crowd into the hole at once. We took turns going to our houses to snitch food—bananas, apples, carrots, slices of watermelon—which we would then divide.

The hole got deeper. The pile of dirt in the alley got higher and higher. Now the entire club could meet in the hole. We needed light, so we took a kerosene lamp underground with us. I don't know why we did not suffocate. We held meetings, discussing our China project. It was better than breaking legs, and Mortzy liked it much better.

---

## Camphor Cures

Keep a stiff upper nose.

—Ish

Once Dad yanked our telephone, wires and all, out of the wall when the number he wanted was repeatedly busy. Another time he peeled a sign that read SCARLET FEVER off our house and went to work, taking himself out of quarantine. To rip and defy seemed part of his nature.

After he saw that the doctors could not make my mother well or even diagnose her illness, he had it in for doctors, even for dentists. If he had a toothache, he would put camphor on a piece of cotton and swab the tooth to kill the pain. He did his own extracting, and ours, too, when necessary, with a pair of pliers or with a doorknob and string by slamming the door.

Camphor was a big item in our house. In the dead of winter, every time I got home after a haircut, I would get a neck rub with camphor "to keep me from getting a cold." It really stung! Once I watched Dad pour a huge bottle of camphor all over Mabel's head, completely soaking her hair and the pillow, to rid her of a bad headache. He just held a towel over her eyes and poured. The headache went away.

He once had what he called a "small accident"—falling off the roof of a three-story house on a windy day. He came home, lay down on his couch in the den, and sent me upstairs to get a shotgun and shells from a locked drawer in his bedroom. Then he dispatched me to the drugstore for a quart bottle of camphor. He kept the gun under the couch, the shells under his pillow. "This shotgun is to shoot any doctor you get foolish enough to call," he said. He lay right next to the phone in the house. Nobody dared touch it.

But there came a day when he was caught half-aware and taken to a hospital after a fall from the eaves of our house onto our cement driveway. After two days in the hospital, he was sent home with this message: "We can't do anything for him. He won't let us near him. Says he can mend himself. Let him!"

Another time, impaled upside down through the thigh on an iron picket fence, he somehow extricated himself (telling those who tried to help him to "get the hell away from me"), crawled to his car, drove home to his couch, submitted to a tetanus shot, and suffered it out. He carried unset broken bones to his grave. He was not a drinking man, but in a fix like that, he would swallow a nip of whiskey "to warm his innards and help kill the pain." And he would smell his camphor.

He bought his camphor by the quart, and in such a large container it was awkward to handle. So he always transferred it into smaller bottles, which he distributed around the house in handy places. So, lying on his couch, he had only to reach out to a windowsill. He would smell the camphor often, to keep "from fainting and because it smells so good." It smelled like he was getting well, he said.

Among the ills he cured in this fashion were minor broken bones, the common cold, fevers, and all aches, including a chronic pain in his side that suggested his appendix was about to burst. A doctor cousin of my mother's, Percy Parsons, stopping by one day to talk to Dad about a new house, cautioned: "Mart, you'd better get that side of yours looked at. It could be serious. If it's your appendix, you could be dead tomorrow." My father shot back: "So I'll be dead, but not cut up!"

He often pounded his side in the middle of the night with his fist. Waking up, I heard that pounding and smelled camphor. When I asked him if the pounding hurt, he said: "Sure it hurts. But it's a different hurt. Makes me forget the other one. Anyway, it's only the Bogue liver."

He and Aunt Flora were always referring to their Bogue liver. I have never known what they meant.

## Cornet in My Hip Pocket

No kid ever stole a bicycle with a mitt in his hip pocket.

—Babe Ruth

Dad loved music, and that is why I had to take piano lessons. He, Mabel, and my teacher conspired to make me practice every day. That lasted for three years, until I was almost twelve. Then I rebelled. I wanted to quit. I said it over and over.

One day Dad and Mabel were talking about Christmas, which was not far off. They asked me if there was something I especially wanted. "What *I* want for Christmas is to quit piano lessons!" I said. The greatest Christmas present I could think of, I continued, would be to be able to go outdoors every day and play ball with the kids.

I thought of Roddie Adams, who lived around the corner from us on Wayne Street. He played cornet in some theater downtown. I had heard he was "a professional." So I asked: "How about a cornet? That's what Roddie Adams plays." But I was not taking all this talk too seriously.

Dan Bryner and I had a new thing afoot. We were going to Lake Erie on secret fishing expeditions in the middle of the night. It was not something we did every night, but we did go at least twice a week, on warm nights. We would wait until our houses quieted down and we could hear snoring—generally about 2 A.M.

Dan lived upstairs over another family directly across the street from us. We had well-laid plans in case I should fall asleep. Since Dan had a small, quiet alarm clock that he kept under his pillow and that no one else could hear, it was certain he would come for me. Once he heard snoring, it was a cinch for him to creep downstairs to the front door. The people living on the first floor slept at the back.

Under my bedroom window Dan would find a lead sinker at the end of a heavy string attached to my big toe. When he pulled on the string two or three times, I was sure to wake up. I had made a rope ladder, which I kept under my mattress. Once I felt Dan's tug and could hear some snoring, too, I would quickly lower the ladder out my window and climb down, and we were off, our fishing gear already in our pockets.

We walked the first few times the whole two miles down to Lake Erie, or, more accurately, to Presque Isle Bay. After that, we rode our bikes. We sat on a rock fishing with our string until dawn was not far off. Then we hustled home. I shinnied up the ladder and crawled into bed about daybreak.

One night, as I stepped over the windowsill into my room, there stood Dad in his nightshirt. I was in for it. But he just put his hand on my shoulder. "Haven't you had enough of this?" he asked. "I've known where you were all this time, Mern. One of the first nights you went, I followed you boys all the way to the lake. When I saw what you were doing, I decided, 'Let 'em alone. They're having fun.' You know, I used to do this sort of thing when I was a boy. But you don't have to sneak down that ladder. You can go out the front door—unless the ladder's more fun. Did you catch anything tonight?" And he went back to bed. After that, we went hardly at all. It was not nearly so much fun for me.

One day I was up in the attic rummaging around, looking at things. I was alone in the house. I found what looked like an interesting case, well hidden. I opened it up. It was a cornet! I fooled around with it, got so I could blow a few notes, and put it all back in place.

Then, on a day when I knew everybody was going out, I asked George Mong, a cousin through Mabel, to sneak up there with me and teach me something about the cornet. He taught me the fingering of the eight-note scale, and over a period of a month of secret trips to the attic, he taught me to play "America."

On Christmas morning I acted surprised to get my present. I took the cornet out of the case, fingered the valves, and, before I realized what I was doing, knocked off a couple of choruses of "America." Dad laughed and said: "Well, Mabel, we've got a genius in the family. He can already play 'My Country 'Tis of Thee.'" Both of them must have known that this was not the first time I had played that cornet. But they never let on, and neither did I. All they said were five words that lighted up my face as bright as the Christmas tree: "You can quit piano lessons!"

This family I had now was not a hugging family. Otherwise I

would have hugged them both. Dad went around town telling all his friends how quickly his twelve-year-old had learned to play the cornet.

---

## KDKA Radio

> Moss is stuff that, if it weren't for rolling stones, nobody would care if they gathered it or not.
>
> —Ish

Roddie Adams practiced his cornet every day, and I could hear him across the back lawns. Roddie was the best in town; he played in the pit at the Columbia Theater. So I took lessons from him at Erie Conservatory of Music. But I would take a while and quit, take a while and quit. I did not know why.

Then I met Oscar Nutter, who played at the Columbia with Roddie. At one time he had played with the Ringling Brothers Circus band. His instrument was trombone. He tried to get me to stay with Roddie. He told me that when I got good enough to play for dances, I could make from three to five dollars a night.

Five dollars a night? It sounded like a bonanza.

He suggested that I come to his house and sit in on the Sunday practice sessions of his small orchestra; he would charge me only fifty cents a Sunday. For about twenty weeks I went. Then I lost interest. I was paying out money instead of taking it in. I still did not see myself ever being part of any musical world. So I quit going to Oscar's.

Besides, the kids who hung around with me were all fired up about a new fad. Actually, history was being made, though I did not realize it then. It was early 1921. There was a new thing you could build that could pick up music right out of the air. For three or four dollars you could buy a kit downtown that consisted of several items, including a crystal—a little square piece of white crystal with an "energy source" in it and a little pinprick needle with a spring on it. The kit provided directions on how to make what was called a radio out of wire and other materials. You got a Mother's Quaker Oats round box—waiting till it was empty, naturally—about four inches in diameter and seven inches long. You skinned copper wire and wrapped it tightly around the box, keeping the wires close together and gluing as you wrapped.

The kit gave you a little gimmick that rode across the top of the box. You could slide this gimmick back and forth across the copper wire that was wound around the box. Its purpose was to tune in different stations. The kit also contained a set of earphones and all the little switches and other necessary dealiebobbies.

Naturally I wanted one. But I did not have the money. Three or four dollars? I cut our grass every week, but I liked to do that. A kid did not get paid for such pleasure, or even ask to be paid. Besides, I didn't need money. Every day my lunch was packed, and I walked the two miles each way to and from school.

I decided that if I wanted the radio kit, I would have to sell a few of my souvenirs that I knew certain kids drooled over: my big ball of string five inches across, my Toronto fair pennant, my crack-and-span steelie, and other loves.

I did not exactly understand the principle behind the radio, but a couple of older kids on the block told me it played music coming from other cities. I was only thirteen, but I could not wait to buy the kit and get the thing built. Handy at woodworking, which I had learned mostly from my father and to some extent from school, I built a wooden box—twelve cubic inches—to mount the radio in, according to the directions, and I worked every spare minute in the den of the old house at 817 East 21st Street. Extending from the dining room toward the backyard, it was a small room that Dad had added as an office for himself.

I told no one about my radio, since I did not know whether it would work. But one night I got it all put together. I tuned it in, I found an energy source on the crystal, and whammo! Here comes somebody talking from Pittsburgh, Pennsylvania, on a station called KDKA, and they are pleading for money for the Milk Fund! They were asking listeners for donations. Apparently they assumed from that end that they were only reaching the area right around Pittsburgh. They seem not to have known how far out their voices were carrying. Later I heard that KDKA had trouble reaching distances because of the mountains around Pittsburgh.

Anyway, I heard KDKA on the earphones that night. I listened for almost an hour. They played marching band music for a while, and then they pleaded again for donations to the Milk Fund, I suppose for poor people.

I was lying on my back on the floor, listening, when Dad came into the room. "What are you doing down there on the floor?" he asked.

"Dad, I'm listening to Pittsburgh on this radio I made!" I answered.

"What do you mean Pittsburgh?"

"Well, there's music and talk coming from Pittsburgh, and I'm listening to it."

He waved me away. "Aw, come on, what do you mean? Why, there's no such thing! You can't hear music and talk through the air with a little thing like that! Pittsburgh to Erie? Why, Mern, that's 150 miles! Somebody's joshing you."

"No, that's what it is. It's called a radio set, and I built it, Dad. I *did.* I put it together according to these directions here. A lot of kids have them, and . . . here, just put these on and listen."

He put the earphones on and, after a minute, took them off. "Aw, pshaw! You got something in that box that's doing that—a record or something."

One could never tell with Dad—he might be needling me, I thought. I told him that KDKA had just got its license to broadcast the October before: "Dad, you must have read something about radio coming!"

"But not homemade, Mern!"

I talked some more about what I had learned concerning KDKA, and I sounded as though I knew what I was talking about. Dad may have believed me. He had to later, when radios began to be manufactured and sold in stores, but that was not for several years. Atwater-Kent put out a red Bakelite set that had three dials that the listener turned to get a whistling tone. The dials had to be turned until the whistle "bottomed out"; when the whistle got to the bottom, you heard voices or music. It was called a superheterodyne radio. How I loved to let that word roll off my tongue! It made me out so knowledgeable. I really was not, of course.

Besides KDKA, we kids were soon listening to the WGY Schenectady Marching Band—a brass band that played live on that station all day long. There was no such thing as playing records on radio in those days.

It was on my little crystal set that I first heard Stoopnagle and Bud. They came from Schenectady, I think, having been born in that area. Little did I dream that one day I would know Stoopnagle. We had that set of mine around the house for a long time. It was not until the mid-1920s or later that radios were available in stores.

I had been taking lessons from Roddie for some time when our church invited me to play my horn in the pulpit one Sunday. Taking lessons from Roddie gave me considerable neighborhood prestige.

What should I play? What would be an appropriate number? I did not ask anybody's advice. I chose "My Blue Heaven" and played two choruses. I played the first chorus straight; the second, I jazzed up—doing it just like Red Nichols would have.

Jazz music in a Methodist church? Back then it simply was not done. But no one criticized me at all, at least not to my face.

When I got into Academy High School, I learned that there was a scarcity of dance cornet men in Erie because so many of the good ones had left for college. I joined the school band, and my cornet got good workouts.

I now listened more carefully to the bands playing on my crystal set, and they were getting to me. Coon Sanders and the Kansas City Nighthawks played a tune called "Here Comes My Ball and Chain." Jean Goldkette's Orchestra from Detroit had a cornet player named Bix Beiderbecke and an alto saxophone player named Frankie Trumbauer. Other bands were Ben Bernie from Chicago, with his "Yowsah, yowsah," and Al Katz and His Kittens. All were part of the beginning of the Big Band Days. And there was also Paul Whiteman.

---

## Bix and Red

> Life is something like this trumpet. If you don't put anything in it you don't get anything out. And that's the truth.
>
> —W. C. Handy

The turning point that set me seriously to work on my cornet occurred when George Gallagher, who owned the Presque Isle

Six, promised to use me on New Year's Eve (I think it was 1924) at the Josephenum if I would "practice up good" and learn to play "hot choruses." He said he would pay me five dollars!

Dad outfitted me with a tuxedo. He rarely gave me money, so I had to earn my own spending money. But he always knew when something was important, and he was generous when it counted.

Oscar Nutter's words kept coming back at me: "When you get good enough to play for dances . . ." I decided to make myself good enough! I practiced every day at home. How did Mabel stand that constant playing upstairs? I will always be grateful that she never once complained.

I bought all Red Nichols' 78 RPM records as fast as they came out. Over and over I played the hot choruses on a Victrola with a hand crank, hundreds of times, until my ear knew exactly what notes were coming next. I practiced along with Red for hours at a time. Then I played along with Red on the whole record, until I could imitate him to a T. I learned his hot choruses on four or five tunes, such as "Sheik of Araby," "Dinah," "Plenty Off Center," and "Back Home in Indiana."

By New Year's Eve I was ready. At the Josephenum I knocked the band's hats off when I played. They said, "Just like Red Nichols." With this reputation, I was approached by Erie bands and asked to join them. Then I learned Bix Beiderbecke's and Louis Armstrong's choruses, and I could play all night with a band in any style they asked me to. "Play like Bix tonight," they would say, and I would be Bix—as nearly as I could, anyway. But who can copy a genius?

Soon I could invent my own choruses on any tune a band happened to be playing, in a sort of Beiderbecke-Nichols style that I made my own. After that, I did not copy anymore.

There were five or six good bands in Erie that played for dances. It was a matter of pride to say you were with this band or that band—to the exclusion of all others—like a loyalty bond. One was not supposed to "play the field." It was as if each band said: "We will use you, but you can't play any single dates with anyone else. You are either with us 100 percent, or we don't want you."

The Presque Isle Six was probably the best band. But I was

not in their league yet. I played with a lot of bands—the Red and Black Melody Boys, for instance, and Harry Rowland. One summer I played with Herbie Johnson at Chautauqua, New York. Years later, when I was doing movies in Hollywood and met Lucille Ball, she told me that as a teenager she had danced to our music at Chautauqua. She lived nearby, in Jamestown, New York.

In those days my goal was to be with the band that had the most jobs lined up. None of the bands had a steady job in a restaurant or a regular spot, not at first. For the most part we worked only Saturday nights, holidays, and summers.

But when I thought I was good enough, I left the bands with occasional jobs and took my first steady job—seven nights a week on the boat *Americana,* which left the dock at the foot of State Street for a lake cruise of two or three hours. It had a sister ship, the *Canadian.* Playing for this dance band meant a fortune to me. I was paid eighty dollars a week, and I played that job for six months. Then I joined the musicians' union and went out of town with Mark Goff and His Club Miami Orchestra, on a tour of theaters in Pennsylvania and Ohio. After I finished high school in 1926, I was freer to go out on the road.

It was through Dick Borel that I got my job with the Presque Isle Six. Dick was playing trumpet for them, and he was going to enter Ohio State University. So when he left, I was hired to take his place.

Dick Borel was an Erie boy, a good man on the trumpet and a good friend of mine. When Ferde Le Jeune came through Erie with his Paul Whiteman SS *Leviathan* Orchestra, I joined him, and we went to Geneva-on-the Lake, near Ashtabula, Ohio. Le Jeune's men had uniforms engraved in gold along the shoulders, and to be part of that band was really something. Ferde needed another trumpet, and so I phoned Borel in Erie and he came over and joined us. We played alongside each other. There was a fellow named Kyser appearing across the street with his own band in a place called the Bird Cage. We did not know him, but we knew he was our competition. Little did I know the role he was going to play in my life.

Dick stayed in Columbus after graduating from Ohio State and managed a top radio (later television) station there—WBNS.

He taught me many crazy routines that I can still rattle off. He would be surprised at how nonchalantly I can speak his absurd, mixed-up languages even today.

The summer before I entered college, a band came through Erie that had formed in Scranton, Pennsylvania, called Fred Waring and His Scranton Sirens (later His Pennsylvanians). They were on one-nighters. They had played one night and had another to go when their trumpet player got sick. (Sometimes one-nighters spilled over into the next night or the next.) Waring called the musicians' union for a replacement, and the union gave him my phone number.

Never having heard of Fred Waring, I checked him out and learned that he had been playing at the Balaban theaters in Chicago and had taken his orchestra to Paris, France. This was in 1927, and he was not famous yet. That came later, after he went on radio in 1933.

Luckily I was at home when Waring called, and I jumped at the chance to play with a traveling band and said I'd be down. After I played that night, Waring asked me if I could go on the road with them. They were booked in Buffalo next. I talked it over with Dad, and he said I could go. But he also said, "What about college?"

After I said good-bye and left with my suitcase, Dad shut the front door and jammed his fist into the wood panel so hard it cracked the wood. Somebody asked him: "What did you do that for? You could have broken your hand!" He just said, "Another one of my kids leaving home forever and I don't like it."

But I was home in three days. Fred said that he knew I was planning to go to college, and so maybe I had better go back to Erie from Buffalo, since it was just a short distance. I did go back. I figured that his cornet player was no longer sick. That was my first brush with a rising celebrity.

## Don Bestor's Boys

Sit, stand, walk, talk, dress and act as though you were the person you want to be ten years from now.
—William J. Reilly

People living through the 1920s did not know that the decade would later be famous as the Roaring Twenties. Sure, there were Prohibition, illegal bathtub gin, and the Charleston. But I have talked with many persons whose attitude is something like this: "I was there, in my twenties myself, but I never roared. I was never in a speakeasy in my life, and I didn't know how to do the Charleston."

But much was happening. The papers were full of stories on such events as the Leopold and Loeb trial, the Scopes trial in Tennessee, and the death of Floyd Collins in a Kentucky cave. Lindbergh flew the Atlantic alone. Movies went from silent films to "talking pictures." And even though radio was in existence throughout the decade, it was not until the late 1920s that the average American family bought one.

In September, 1926, when Tunney won over Dempsey in the heavyweight championship fight in Philadelphia, my sister and her husband, on a honeymoon-business trip courtesy of Procter and Gamble, traveled through a small Pennsylvania town and heard the fight over a loudspeaker radio mounted on a truck in the main street of the town. Many hundreds of people gathered to listen. Practically the whole population of the town and the surrounding area was said to be there.

In the fall of 1927 I entered West Virginia University to study law. I played with the Reece Henry Orchestra to help with my expenses, mostly on Friday and Saturday nights for college dances. Once in a while I played with Al Mabey's Orchestra. A musician did not have to be "loyal" down there—it was grab as grab can.

In June I returned to Erie to play with Mendel Jones at the Cameo Restaurant at 10th and Peach. We played three sessions a day—noon to 2 P.M., 6 to 8 P.M. for dinner, and 9 P.M. to midnight for dancing.

Before long we heard that Guy Lombardo was coming to the Cameo for three nights. Guy was well-known in Cleveland at that time. He had come from Canada and was playing at the Music Box in Cleveland. He would play for six or eight months, then go out on one-nighters, and then return to the Music Box. One of the engagements he booked was at Erie's Cameo, which meant that Mendel Jones and the rest of us had three days' vacation.

A big party for Guy was planned at the Cameo. A long table was set for his band and for our band members, wives, and dates. It was at the Guy Lombardo party that I met Janet Meade. She sat at the long table with her date, and I sat nearby with mine. There she was—a vision in white—and I flipped my cap! When I got a chance, I arranged to be introduced to her and then asked for a dance. That's the way it was done in those days! Guy's music began, and my whole world came up roses and apple pie.

We made plans while dancing. Janet would go home early, and I would take my girl home early. She would get out of the car in front of her house, where she would wait till I came along, and we would have what we came to call "a late date."

You think because Ish Kabibble puts on a dumb face on the stage that he's really dumb? No sir, not me! I know a future bride when I see one!

Janet came by her love of the musical world naturally. Her father, Charles Meade, was a professional musician who played violin with the Cleveland Symphony Orchestra; he also directed his own orchestra in theaters during the silent-movie years. He directed the Empire Theater Orchestra in Cleveland. The Empire was a burlesque theater, which was something to be proud of then, as in those days burlesque was not a cheap show. It was musical comedy at its best; some of our most famous comedians started in burlesque.

Janet's family included her witty mother, Effie, and a sister, Frances, who added to the Meade renown by graduating from college Phi Beta Kappa. Effie Meade used expressions right out of the cracker barrel, such as, "Every tub should sit on its own bottom." If you saw a leftover cupcake on her shelf and asked, "What's that?" hoping to be offered it, Effie would say, "That's a layover to catch a meddler."

The big thing that happened in the late 1920s was the Stock Market Crash of 1929. I lost fourteen dollars—all I had to my name. I had put it in a bank in Morgantown, and when I went down to draw it out, I stood in a long line. The guy right in front of me got inside, but the door was shut in my face. That bank never opened its doors again, and my fourteen dollars was gone forever. That fourteen dollars meant as much to me as fourteen hundred dollars might to another man or fourteen thousand to a rich one. It was my nest egg.

I went home for Christmas that December. Money was tight for everyone. A could not pay B, B could not pay C, and so on down to X, Y, and Z. On Christmas morning we all waited until everyone was up, and then we marched to the tree and got our presents. The Crash had stamped its mark at the base of the tree; there was a noticeable scarcity of packages. The floor looked bare. We all had about three packages apiece. But we had a good time opening them, and slippers and gloves were too small and too large, just like in other years.

After I had spent two years at West Virginia University and had played both years with the Reece Henry Orchestra, Reece asked me if I wanted to join him in playing with Don Bestor and His Orchestra for the summer at the William Penn Hotel in Pittsburgh. Bestor had asked Reece to suggest a second trumpet player.

I accepted the offer, and Reece and I shared a room at the Pittsburgh YMCA. Bestor's orchestra was the first "big band" that I played for that had a radio broadcast. It broadcast every day at noon from the hotel over station KDKA. "KDKA! I'm playing over KDKA!" I kept telling myself. I could hardly believe it, remembering my little homemade crystal set still in use at home. That summer I was paid a hundred dollars a week—big dough! But our expenses were high.

In the fall Don did not want me to leave to go back to school and asked if I would stay with him another semester—until the following February. This I did, because I liked playing for Don and I needed the money. We played in the Italian Room at the William Penn Hotel. There was much prestige associated with playing with Don Bestor. He wanted all his men to act and look like gentlemen and be a credit to him at all times. He was not only particular about how they looked on the bandstand, but he went one step further, controlling what they wore off duty. In the daytime, if you were seen around town, you had to be dressed in a Chesterfield overcoat, with a small velvet collar (such as was worn with a tuxedo), a black derby, and gray spats, and you had to carry a cane. Even our shoes were all alike—patent leather. Don wanted people on the street to say, with respect and admiration, "There goes one of Don Bestor's boys."

Such control over a band's appearance was an innovation in musicians' circles. I know of no other band leader who ever went so far in dictating how his boys should look offstage. Whenever we entered the William Penn Hotel, we were to use the main entrance—no side doors. We were to walk through the main lobby to be viewed by hotel customers, who, Don hoped, would say, "There go the Don Bestor boys to work." We had a dressing room on the second floor where we changed into our tuxedos. It was a matter of pride for me to play with Don Bestor.

When we got a break between dances, we were supposed to do what was called "make the tables." We were assigned certain tables in the room and were to introduce ourselves to the customers. "Good evening! I am Merwyn Bogue, and I play the trumpet," I would say. We hoped to be invited to sit down and talk with the people and get acquainted. This practice tended to bring customers back time and again, because they got to know various boys in the band. It was good for business and increased the chances that the band would be asked to play that hotel again.

In February, when I went back to West Virginia University, I had a good feeling inside from my experience with Don Bestor's band. I had not been back at school long when Dad phoned to ask if I could come home for a couple of days. He wanted to talk with me, he said. I was mystified, but I knew he would never make such a request without a good reason.

When I got home, I found him cleaning his gun. That gave me a jolt, since the Crash had occurred only about three months before and men all over the country were using guns to get rid of themselves.

"Hi, Dad. So you're cleaning that old gun of yours," I said, sitting down on the back-door steps beside him.

"Yeah. I haven't had a day off in years to clean this thing right." It was the gun that had kept us from calling a doctor in the past.

"Now my hunting guns—I clean those immediately as soon as I get home from a hunting trip." Hunting was his second love; building was his first. He motioned to the rattletrap car I had left in the drive. "Is that the thing you bought for thirty dollars?"

"That's it, and it brought me all the way up here. It doesn't look like much, does it?"

"No, it doesn't." He laughed. "Hope it gets you back."

"It has to. By the time I paid my tuition and room and board, the Bestor money was gone."

I waited. He had some trouble getting started, but finally he said: "I've been dreading to tell you this, Mern, but I had to file bankruptcy papers a week or so ago. Everything I had is gone."

Bankrupt? My dad? I couldn't believe it. A few years before, he had gone into the gas-and-oil business, wholesale and retail. He built half a dozen gas stations around Erie and bought gas and oil by the carload, since he had his own railroad siding near his lumber yard. The last I had heard he was dickering with a national oil company that was interested in buying him out—all the gas stations, houses, and lots. Dad and Will, his partner, were to get a price in six figures.

"I never told you this, Mern, but shortly before the Crash the oil company backed out. Maybe they got scared, or maybe it was because Will wanted to hold out for more money. I wanted to sell. But anyway, the company backed out. You know I've been carrying people on my books for years, letting them charge gas and oil. The men running the gas stations got behind in their payments, and we carried them. What could we do? We'd known these customers, some of them, all our lives, and they'd plead for time. And times have been so hard that a lot of families buying my houses couldn't meet payments. I owed the banks, of course, had borrowed up to my limit. When the banks called in their loans, I was caught. I lost everything, Mern." He looked at the ground and gave the grass a kick.

I was so mad about what had happened to him that I could not think of what to say. He was a proud man, proud of having made it on his own, and he had reason to be. But now, because other people could not pay, he was losing even his house, which he had built with his own hands.

He pulled a small, handwritten card out of his pocket. "Here's what I'm doing about it. It's a comedown for me, but it's the only thing I can do." The card read: "M. H. Bogue. Fixer. Repair work of all kinds. Porches, steps, leaky roofs, small paint jobs. Strictly cash." And it had his address and phone number.

I could not speak. I was so proud of him. He was busted flat, but not bellyaching. There was something he could do well, and he was doing it. He said: "I take these cards around with me house to house every day. I've had some work, and I'll get more. People know me."

"Why, Dad, I had no idea. Why didn't you tell me? I would've quit school. I see now what you were trying to say last fall when I came home and you said you'd give me all your vacant lots if I could pay the taxes on them. You were in trouble then. But Dad, I didn't know what you were saying. I guess I just let it run off my back. I'm sorry. I know it sounds empty to say it now, but I'm sorry."

Dad threw up his hands. "Well, that's all over the dam now. But I feel bad that I can't help you through school anymore. Here I am. I thought I was fixed for life, could educate all my children. And I can't even help you anymore. I can't send Jim or Christine to college. And you know how I feel about an education."

Jim and Christine were Dad and Mabel's children. I knew how he felt about them, and about education, too. He was always wishing he had never quit school. But I tried to make him see that going to college is not all that important. A good part of it is prestige, and my dad had that just from being the kind of person he was. It is what one makes of his life, with college or without, that counts. "To me," I told him, "you're a great man, and you've done it all yourself."

He asked me if I thought I could manage, with my playing, to finish college. "I don't want you to quit to help me," he said, "although I know you would. That's not why I sent for you. I just wanted to explain things. If you had to leave school because of money . . ." He stopped and swallowed a couple of times. It was breaking him up. I said I could finish college by playing my horn—"the horn you bought me."

"Now, let's take a walk," I suggested. "Come on, let's put that thing away!" I said, pointing to the gun. We went upstairs and put it under lock and key.

Later that day, I went upstairs, and with an old jackknife I picked the lock, took out the gun and shells, and snapped the drawer shut. When I had a chance, I drove down to the end of the dock at the foot of State Street and threw the gun and shells as far out into the bay as I could.

I thought he would miss the gun soon. But it was two years before he said: "Remember the day we put that gun into that drawer upstairs? It isn't there now. Do you know anything about it?"

"Yeah, I know where it is. It's at the bottom of the lake, and it's been there for two years."

He looked surprised and then laughed. "Oh, well, now I know where it is. That's OK. I never used the thing anyway except to keep doctors away."

---

## No Moustache, No Whiskey

> Not many sounds in life, and I include all urban and rural sounds, exceed in interest a knock at the door.
>
> —Charles Lamb

Between studying and trying to make enough money to stay in college, I did not have much free time—not even enough to feel sorry for myself because I could not see Janet Meade often enough. Her family had moved back to Cleveland, so even though I occasionally did get to Erie, I did not see Janet. But she was in my head, and we wrote letters.

In the summer of 1930 I joined Hogan Hancock's Orchestra at the Plaza Restaurant in Pittsburgh. From there we moved on to Crystal Beach, Canada, across the lake from Erie. Returning, I had a wreck in Schenectady, which discombobulated my Ford and gave me pains I had been taught to ignore. In exchanging identifications with the driver of the other car, I discovered we were both members of the musicians' union. He was then director of the WGY Schenectady Marching Band, which I used to listen to on my little crystal set. So it's a small world.

At the end of the spring semester, Hal Kemp's Orchestra came to Morgantown to play our big dance. Kemp was very popular. His orchestra was one of the up-and-coming big bands. I went to the dance stag, to hear Kemp. When the time came for him to start, 9 P.M., it turned out that his trumpet player had not shown up. (I should give thanks for sick trumpet players.) Kemp's drummer played a loud drum roll for attention. He called out, "Is there a trumpet player in the hall?"

"I'm one!" I yelled at him. I was standing approximately under his nose. He asked if I considered myself good enough to sit in for the sick man.

"Yes, I am! Be right back!" I ran out of the gymnasium, up High Street to the Sigma Chi house, grabbed my horn, fled back to the gym, and played the whole evening. I sight-read all their tricky arrangements and won the admiration of Hal and his boys. Hal paid me, I think, twenty-five dollars and complimented me on a good job, and that was that. They left town that night, and I went home to bed extra happy.

Exams and classes were over the end of May. I had only a year, or a little more, to go for my B.A. degree. Somewhere, about this time, Hal Kemp ran into Kay Kyser, who needed a trumpet player. Hal told Kyser about "this Bogue." Kyser sent me a telegram:

CLEVELAND OHIO
6/3/31

MERWYN BOGUE
SIGMA CHI FRATERNITY
WEST VIRGINIA UNIVERSITY
MORGANTOWN, WEST VIRGINIA
UPON RECOMMENDATION OF HAL KEMP LIKE TO HAVE YOU TRY OUT WITH MY BAND FIRST TRUMPET AT WILLOWS OAKMONT PENNSYLVANIA JUNE FIFTEENTH REHEARSAL STOP SALARY OPEN STOP FIRM RULES ABSOLUTELY NO MOUSTACHES, NO WHISKEY STOP MUST BE CLEAN CUT STOP ANSWER BY RETURN WIRE BAMBOO GARDENS CLEVELAND OHIO

KAY KYSER

Pleased as I was, I did not take it seriously at first. I had never considered quitting school. If I were accepted by Kyser, it would probably mean no degree. I needed to think it over.

That night, at a friend's house, who should come on the radio but Kay Kyser from the Bamboo Gardens in Cleveland? I pulled the telegram from my pocket, and some of the guys thought I should accept. The band sounded good to me. I went home to bed but could not sleep. A few things bothered me.

I was facing another year of having to earn all necessary money for tuition, room and board, and other expenses. I could probably do it, but there was something else. The university band members had just elected me their drum major for the coming year, and as such, I was supposed to twirl the baton. By fall I was supposed to be adept at it. But I had never tried to twirl a baton until the past day or so, and I was not catching on. Besides, it was not *me*. The thought of me out there on a field twirling a baton did not seem to fit. I saw myself only with my horn. I squirmed and tossed the whole night. It would be quite a humiliation if I finally had to admit I could not twirl—or did not even want to.

How could I do it? Give up the rest of my college education, give up the study of law—did I really *want* to study law?—just because I was not a natural-born baton twirler? Ridiculous! Why not swallow my pride, stay, let a good baton twirler twirl, and get my degree?

But there was a glamour to band work that I loved. Lying there in bed, I saw myself onstage, saw myself traveling with a band, and I got so excited that I had to get up and walk the floor.

Who ever heard of a trumpet-playing lawyer?

How I loved my horn! But how would Dad feel?

In the morning I telephoned him, and we had a good talk. He said it was up to me. He seemed pleased, I thought. So I sent my I WILL BE THERE telegram to Kay Kyser. I was twenty-three years old.

When I arrived in Oakmont on June 15 and looked up Kay, he greeted me with his warm southern hospitality and then said: "I'm glad to meet you, because you look like a gentleman, and my credo is that I'd rather hire a gentleman and make a musician out of him than hire a musician and try to make a gentleman out of him. So now if you'll join the band over there in the first-trumpet chair, we'll find out if you're a musician."

Kay's arranger, George Duning, had arranged one of the trickiest introductions to a song I had ever seen, but I played it without error, to the complete amazement of the whole band. Kay held up his hands. "OK, that's enough! You're in!"

So that is how I came to join Kay Kyser and how I came not to graduate from West Virginia University after finishing three years. It was not easy to leave. Wherever we go, we leave a little and we take a little. As Alfred Tennyson wrote, "I am a part of all that I have met."

# 2

## THE 1930s
## THE RISE OF ISH

## The Depression

Old Mother Hubbard went to her cupboard
To get her poor dog a bone;
She found the bone on the very top shelf,
But it looked so good she ate it herself.

—Ish

The question is often asked, What instrument did Kay Kyser play? The answer is none. He was not primarily a musician. He was, however, two things that made up for it. He was an outstanding businessman and a natural showman. I think he was one of the first ever to lead organized cheering at college football games, something he did at the University of North Carolina. And he was a master at disciplining a band.

When we left the Willows that fall and were booked into the Bamboo Gardens at 102nd and Euclid in Cleveland, it was a return engagement for Kay, but no one in the band was any happier than I was. For Janet Meade now lived in Cleveland with her parents, and she was working within three blocks of the Bamboo Gardens. For five whole months Janet and I spent all our available evenings after work with band members and their wives. Late dates!

After a short month of one-nighters on the road, the band was back in Cleveland in April, booked this time into the Golden Pheasant Restaurant. Perfect timing for two lovebirds.

On May 9, 1932, Janet and I were married in Cleveland in the Old Stone Church on the Downtown Square. Our wedding day was smack dab in the middle of the Great Depression. Bands and businesses of all kinds were folding. We were glad to have jobs. Dollars were so scarce that I had to finance Janet's ten-dollar wedding ring—fifty cents down and twenty-five cents a week. That's how bad it was. It was the depression. You need to have been there to truly understand it.

At the church an unexpected delay nearly wrecked the time schedule. The band had taken their instruments, intending to play the wedding march as we left the church. But when the minister spotted the instruments hidden in the pews, he insisted they be removed before he started the ceremony. Saxophones and such in a church? It just was not done.

The Golden Pheasant Restaurant, where the band was playing and where we had our reception and luncheon after the 11 A.M. ceremony, was practically paying us in the form of food—chop suey for breakfast, egg foo yong for lunch, noodles for dinner. Relatives and friends came from as far away as New York, and the whole band was there. But just married or not, I had to play the noon session.

Now life was perfect. Poor? What did we care? Now when the band went out on one-nighters, Janet could go with me.

It was not unusual in those hard times for someone in a small town to promote a dance for which our pay was to be a certain percentage of the take. We might get 60 percent, the promoter 40 percent. That was one way a person out of a job could make a little money.

We sometimes had to haggle for cash. One organizer of a dance in the Midwest wanted to pay us in books he had written. "But you could sell them!" he cried.

More than one promoter tried to get away with the whole 100 percent. One night we were playing the last dance of the evening when Sully Mason and I noticed that the booth at the entrance door where the promoter, who was a farmer, had been standing was deserted. The second we played the last note, we both ran to the doorway. No farmer. Outside, we saw him hotfooting it across a field of corn stubble. We took after him in leaps and bounds and caught him. He had his cigar box full of money under his arm. In the moonlight we counted out the agreed amount due Kay and let the guy go. But Sully and I had sore ankles and shins for a long time.

"There is something to be said for depressions," wrote Russell Lynes in *Harpers* magazine in 1956. "There is nothing to be said for the evils depressions produce, for empty stomachs and ruined houses, for bread lines and broken families, and the terror of not having a job. There is a great deal to be said for the climate they produce, a climate in many respects more productive than prosperity—more interesting, more lively, more thoughtful and even in a wry sort of way, more fun. . . . [But, more important,] a depression not only gives people time to think, it makes them think. . . . Men and women are not only more ingenious about entertaining themselves, they are more thoughtful about work." And I suppose there is even something to be said for sore ankles and shins. They are better than sore feet.

---

## Fifty Cents Short

> Shoulders is things that if you didn't have any, you wouldn't have nothin' to shrug with.
>
> —Ish

To this point in my life I had heard of slack periods but had never suffered one. Before I joined Kay, if I had a period without work, I simply went home until I got another offer. Now I learned that it was common for a rising young band to have times of unemployment. In fact, it was one of the problems of the business.

Few radio listeners or television viewers, as they sit enjoying successful top-rated groups or single performers, have any conception of the tough days that brought these people to where they are. A successful self-made performer, whatever heights he may reach in his profession, can never erase from his thoughts all the early days of hard work and disappointment, the weeks and months with little money, the meals skimped on or skipped. There were times when we even had to count pennies.

In the early 1930s, when the Kyser band could afford only ten of us, we knew what it was to be poor. If, when we finished an engagement in one part of the country, we had no work for a few weeks until we were to open in another part, then just the basic cost of living hurt. Although the band furnished transportation from one job to another, the members had to pay their own eating and sleeping costs, which would often eat up all the cash in our pockets. That was when we felt the pinch of poverty and when we looked for a box of cookies or fudge from home.

We combed the Midwest on one-nighters: Jimmy Peppe's Valley Dale in Columbus, Coney Island in Cincinnati, Kansas City, Memphis, and St. Paul, with slack periods thrown in. In early 1933 we played several weeks in Albany, New York, at the Albany Hotel. One of our well-known nightly customers was Legs Diamond. He had his regular table, off in a corner. He would accept no other. Mr. Diamond occupied the corner chair in a corner of the room, so that no one could ever get behind him.

While we were in Albany, we helped to celebrate the end of one of America's famous eras. During the election campaign of 1932, both political parties came out in favor of repeal of the Eighteenth Amendment. No matter who was elected, Hoover or Roosevelt, Prohibition was sure to die. Although repeal was endorsed by Congress in February, 1933, it took the states until December to ratify the new amendment. But right after his inauguration, Roosevelt, impatient, appealed to Congress to legalize 3.2 percent beer immediately. It took Congress only nine days to comply. So it was in March, while our band was playing in Albany, when people rejoiced at the end of Prohibition and "beer flowed freely through the streets," as it was said, though I did not go outside to look.

At the end of our Albany engagement, we faced thirty days of unemployment before our next opening in San Francisco at the Bal Tabarin. That month was probably the band's lowest point financially. For us that was when the Great Depression was at its worst, though nobody called it that until years later. Everyone in the band had a serious financial problem. Some of the boys had small children. I was having my first experience as a provider for two. How could we all manage for thirty days without money?

Kay came through with a solution. Not wanting any of his boys to become discouraged, he invited us to drive to his hometown, Rocky Mount, North Carolina. Car expense was paid by the band. We paid our own hotel and food. Once in Rocky Mount, each couple or family was assigned and made welcome in the home of one or more of Kay's relatives or friends. Janet and I stayed with Kay's sister Virginia, and we thoroughly enjoyed her generous hospitality. With the food and comfort and that wonderful southern sense of leisure, we were living again.

Kay organized and promoted a big dance that was held in a huge tobacco warehouse in Rocky Mount, and it brought in enough money for us to start our trip west. A one-nighter in Chester, West Virginia, also helped.

After that dance, Earl Bailey, our manager, called us together, divided all the available funds, and told us to meet three days later in Rock Springs, Wyoming, to play a dance upstairs over the local American Legion hall—a 1,600-mile jump.

Our weary gang all made it, but attendance at the dance was low, and our financial situation was now critical. Earl apportioned the available funds again, and we took off for the Bal Tabarin in San Francisco, nine hundred miles away.

Everyone knew we would never make it on the funds given us. Janet and I were given twenty-five dollars for gas and oil. No one else was better off. So collect telegrams spread across the country to parents and other relatives, pleading for help.

Janet and I had almost made it to Sacramento when we found our gas tank reading "E." We pulled into a gas station, and down to our last resort, we broke open our piggy bank. Gas was around twenty cents a gallon, oil thirty-five cents a quart. It was serious, but we got silly as we counted pennies and nickels. We had less than three dollars. That took us to the waters of San Francisco Bay and to the ferry boat, but the fifty-cent fare for the boat was beyond our means. So we sat at the ferry waiting for part of our gang to catch up, hoping they would have an extra fifty cents.

As we sat waiting, we wondered what day it was, and realized that our first wedding anniversary was almost at hand. How had the year gone by so fast? I asked Janet what she would like for an anniversary present. The question almost sent her into hysterics. "Obviously, I'd like fifty cents! Or maybe a Lorna Doone." The poor kid! Her favorite cookie. I stretched my neck, looking up and down the street for some sort of store.

I spotted one, but when I went in and asked for Lorna Doones, I never expected this tinhorn store to have any. To my surprise, it did. One box took every penny we had left plus three postage stamps.

To this day, wherever we are on May 9, we eat Lorna Doones with much sentiment and gusto. But that day at the ferry, we laughed until we had to hold our stomachs. I said: "It's not fair at all. I'll bet Lorna Doone is loaded with money, and here we sit contributing our last cent to this dame who doesn't need it, and we're not even acquainted with her. We're nothing but her profit."

We chewed our cookies, wishing our water had not run out, and then Muddy Berry, our drummer, drove up. He had sixty cents. "Here," he said, "I'm not even using them." Good old Muddy!

In San Francisco, Earl Bailey and his wife, Mary Kay, teamed up with Janet and me on an ingenious plan. With less than nothing in cash between us and next payday seven days off, we checked into an exceptionally good hotel where we hoped to sleep and eat for a week without money.

We spruced ourselves up pretty sharp before approaching the hotel manager. We asked him if we could sign tabs in the dining room until the end of the week. "Certainly, gentlemen!" he replied. We would be working at the Bal Tabarin; to him that was a good recommendation.

The four of us existed the whole first week without cash. At least Janet and I had none at all. At the end of the week we got paid, settled our hotel bill, and checked out, and the Baileys and the Bogues rented a modest two-bedroom apartment that we shared for the first few months at the Bal. We had a ball—the Baileys, my Janet, and I.

There were times when we were so happy we forgot to feel poor. But those were poor days. Sometimes I would say to Janet, "If somebody gave us time off to take a small trip, we couldn't even get out of sight!"

---

## Flavor of the Times

Nostalgia isn't what it used to be.

—Peter De Vries

"What was it like in those days, Ish? You were there. Tell us, what expressions did you use, what dances did you do?" These were Rice University students talking. It was 1974, and I was based in Houston, selling Colorado ski resort land, and the students were pressing me for details about the Big Band Era. They were taking a summer course in the history of the period between the end of World War I and the beginning of World War II.

I had to dig to remember. "Oh, we said things like 'twenty-three skiddoo,' 'the snake's hips,' 'the cat's meow,' 'Zowie!' 'Yikes!' and 'Whooa, Nellie!'"

"What about 'Joe sent me'?" one of them asked. So I told them about the little window in the speakeasy where you whispered "Joe sent me" to get in. I told them about the Erie speakeasy and the Rhythm Boys and me.

"Wait—wait till I get this all down!" one said. Another asked, "Whatever happened to *you*?" That stumped me for a few seconds until they all laughed. "Hey, man. Where did you ever get a name like Ish Kabibble?"

They did not give me time to answer.

"What dances did you do?"

"Oh, the bunny hug, camel walk, varsity drag, black bottom, Charleston . . ."

"Do some for us!"

"Wait, kids. *I* didn't dance then. I played for people who did, for people huddled around the bandstand. Half the dancers gathered around the orchestra in those days, arms around each other, moving together just enough to hold their rhythm, trying to maneuver into a front-row position."

The students acted as though this whole story was new to them, as if their parents had not been telling it to them probably all their lives. But they had not been listening.

Most of the time those early days were rough rather than glamorous, even though today nostalgia makes it seem that the Big Band Days were an almost magical era. But sometimes it was just plain dull, waiting for late transportation, checking luggage and instruments to be sure everything was on board, trying to get comfortable, trying to sleep while the bus jiggled.

From one one-nighter to another, we traveled mostly in buses. Some of the guys tended to hang around the bus stop too long. An extra cup of coffee could make us late for our next job. So we set up a system by which one of us, when it came time to pull out, would stand with one foot on the bus step and yell out "Hiddle-i-bee!" loud and clear. When the boys heard that, they moved. Hiddle-i-bee meant, "Last call, no time left, run like hell, the bus is moving out." The bus would actually be inching along. It meant: "Move, boy! Git!" Nobody wanted to be left behind at some desert stop or out in the boondocks. Nobody wanted to lose his job.

Although it was a time of the birth of the big bands, I was not aware that I was a part of any special era. Life was mainly hard work and also pranks and practical jokes pulled to counter the humdrum routine of daily rehearsals, work, travel, eating, sleeping. It is difficult to count and classify the trees when you're standing in the middle of the forest, or to judge the extent of hard times when you're living them. I never tried to recognize what parts of our experiences might turn out to be significant in the long run. Bands were formed, flashed in the pan, and disappeared. At any given time it was impossible to predict what band would be around a few weeks later.

Even before I joined Kay, I always decided my next step without much thought as to where each step would lead me or whether it would be fruitful. In the late 1920s, by actual count, I joined and quit more than twenty-eight Dixieland groups. I would stay a few weeks or months and quit. Wise or not, what I was doing was collecting bands, so that when I was sitting around talking with other musicians and they would mention a band, I could say, "Oh, I played with him!" I suppose I felt it gave me stature.

But one day I looked at my bank account, and there was nothing there. So I said to myself, "The very next band you go with, you stick with through thick and thin, better or worse, and see what happens."

It was not long after that that Kay's telegram arrived. I was with Kay for twenty years, longer than any other member of the band. I was with Kay until he retired, and so I was with him for his whole career except for his first four years.

In 1938 I had been with Kay for several years and he had the Lucky Strike radio program and was booked into the Pennsylvania Hotel Roof in New York, but it was still hard for me to have any perspective on the times. Bands were still struggling to stay alive. Hard times were still the talk of the town. As for who had a chance to be famous or what might happen to any single band, I had no time for such analyses. I was too busy wanting our band to be the best, and I was playing trumpet, acting as band manager, and trying to improve my little comedy act.

So when in 1938 I was invited night after night to go with some of the other band members across the street to hear "that fantastic new band," Glenn Miller and His Orchestra, I never seemed able to find the time to go. There was no particular reason. He was not famous yet, and I probably figured that in a few weeks he would be out of the big band picture. It seems hard to believe now. But that's the way it was.

There are figures that support my lack of interest in Glenn Miller in 1938, though they do not excuse it. From 1938 through 1941, *Billboard* magazine conducted annual polls among college students who selected their favorite bands and their favorite band singers. In 1938 the first five bands chosen were those of Benny Goodman, Tommy Dorsey, Hal Kemp, Guy Lombardo, and Kay Kyser. In 1939 the first two were Artie Shaw's and Kay Kyser's. In 1940 the first two were Glenn Miller's and Kay Kyser's. In 1941 the first three bands were those of Glenn Miller, Tommy Dorsey, and Kay Kyser, and Ginny Simms of the Kay Kyser Band was voted top female vocalist.

In neither 1938 nor 1939 was Glenn Miller one of the first five picked. It was not until 1940 that he skyrocketed. And he kept his top spot for a long time, as everyone knows. Of course, I am making an assumption that such a college poll is indicative of general popularity, and that may or may not be correct.

My not making time to cross the street in 1938 does not mean I never went anywhere. In the late 1930s, Janet and I went many times to hear Guy Lombardo at New York's Roosevelt Hotel. We would dance and think back on the time we danced to his music in Erie the first night we met. Sometimes we stopped at his bandstand and asked him to play a number he had played in Erie, but in many cases he did not remember the tune or had long since thrown away the music. "Not playing that anymore!" he would say, laughing. But that was always OK. We just kept right on dancing to Guy Lombardo through the years.

Another place in New York we often went was Nick's, in

Greenwich Village. Nick's was a roomy restaurant owned by a man named Nick Ronghetti. He served sizzling steaks and had long been known for his Dixieland music. Anybody over thirty-five today who likes Dixieland and has ever spent time in New York has probably been to Nick's. When we went there, it was Bobby Hackett's band that played. He played a fantastic trumpet, and there was Peewee Russell on clarinet and Georg Brunis on trombone. Nick was a longtime sponsor of what we used to call Dixieland jazz. He was also a piano player and had two pianos onstage, one for the band and the other for him when he felt like joining in.

Those boys were real artists. Peewee Russell was a great clarinet player, a great favorite of mine, and he had the look of a natural clown. I always considered it a great honor when they asked me to sit in with them, which was not very often. But occasionally they did. Today I get gooseflesh just thinking about it!

---

## The Silver Dollar Trapeze

I sneezed a sneeze into the air.
It fell to earth I know not where.
But you shoulda seen the looks on those
In whose vicinity I snoze.

—Ish

In 1933 Tom Gerun and Frank Martinelli, two outstanding and understanding gentlemen, owned and operated the Bal Tabarin, the famous restaurant and dance spot on Columbus Avenue in San Francisco. (I believe the name of the place was later changed to Bimbo's.) These two fun-loving gentlemen provided the opportunity that not only started the Kay Kyser Band on its way up but also proved to be the turning point in my life that led to many of the good things that were destined to happen to me.

I believe that the course of one's life is often the result of happenstance. You just happen to be in a certain place at a certain time, and something happens that later turns out to have been overwhelmingly important. It was a chance event at the Bal that put the name Ish Kabibble on me. As I said before, I never meant to take it.

The Bal floor show consisted of a line of eight dancing girls plus whatever entertainment the band could muster as its contribution. At that time our band did not have much extra show material. We concentrated on our music and our male singers.

Frank Martinelli decided he would create something new to entertain his customers. Walter O'Keefe, a nationally known humorist of those days, had recorded a song called "The Daring Young Man on the Flying Trapeze," and the record was a hit that was played all over the nation on radio. One day at rehearsal Frank pointed his finger at me and said: "Hey, you, come out here on the floor with me. You're going to sing this song in the floor show tonight, and it's going to fracture the audience."

Within a few minutes his carpenter had drilled two holes in the ceiling above the bandstand and was lowering a rope through the holes to form a trapeze. A small wooden pole was added as a "seat" for me. With help I was hoisted onto that pole. Wow, it hurt! Could my scrawny rump take it? I was skinny; that's probably why Frank chose me. But Frank was kind-hearted. He eased my pain by adding a colorful, red-spangled pillow that changed my expression.

He ordered a costume from a local outfitter. My get-up consisted of form-fitting red tights, curled-up gold slippers with tinkling bells suspended in the air, and a bright yellow-and-gold vest with spangled buttons and beads. Over this went a flimsy, circusy robe with a long train that dragged behind me on the floor as I made my entrance.

Frank handed me a set of lyrics and said: "Memorize this by showtime tonight. You're going to make your debut to all San Francisco as the Man on the Flying Trapeze. And will those people love it! I know my San Francisco audiences."

San Francisco audiences have always been fantastically appreciative. Heavy applause greeted my entrance onto the stage. I peeled off the skimpy robe, and the people cheered when they saw my red tights and garish vest. Holding the robe out for all to see, I flicked a lint or two off with my fingers and dropped the robe casually onto the floor as though it were nothing to me—like an actress dropping her mink.

Moseying over to my trapeze, my tall and skinny self shivered inside my red tights. Gingerly I sat on the pole. But wait—the pillow! I couldn't go without my pillow! Scared and shaking and hurting, I allowed the blessed thing to be inserted under my rear, but then I fell off the trapeze and needed help to get back on. The audience was rolling by now. Whee! Up I went toward the ceiling, much too fast.

Immediately I felt weak, but my music was starting up, and I was supposed to sing my song. I kept wobbling on the swing and could hardly get the words out—those that I could remember. Part of the time I hummed. But the audience not only liked my "frightened" version of the song; they thought the whole thing was intentional—part of the act. I could not sing anyway. One person said I had a voice that sounded like a woodpecker trying to open a can of beer. Someone else thought it was like the rip of a rag.

In a week or so, the audiences were applauding so long I had to go back for encores. In time I made up other lyrics to keep the song fresh. But finally it became ridiculous. I went back so many times that I was stopping the show and could not get off. Was I having fun!

But Kay said enough was enough. After about four months, it was decided I would have to switch to a different song so the audiences would not call me back. My orders were "Be terrible!" After all, we had our dancing girls and our regular singers—all terrific—Sully Mason, Bill Stoker, and Art Wilson.

All during the many encores demanding more "trapeze," the audience would throw silver dollars onto the stage. That was San Francisco's way of saying, "We like you." But when the dancers came out to dance, some of them tripped on the coins and fell, so the boss had to order the waiters to run onto the darkened stage with wide brooms and sweep the dollars off before the dancers came on.

The waiters got the dollars. Who was to tell them no? Whose dollars were they? No rule answered that. Neither did any rule stipulate that the waiters were to sweep the dollars into piles and leave them. But it got to the point that there were more dollars on the stage than I earned in a week. In those days we were not exactly the highest paid workers in the world. Sure, I yearned to pocket some, but that would have been unpardonable. You just did not do that—not in the Bal Tabarin, a class night club.

But I was human. Some guys were taking some pretty big tips they had not earned. One day I had an idea that I felt might amuse the audiences while causing me no harm either. I bought several yards of material and used it to extend the length of my robe. Now when I shed the robe and dropped it, I tossed it around a little until it covered most of the dance floor—just a casual flip, understand.

The audiences were way ahead of me, cheering and stomping. They were indeed my friends. Now when they threw money, they tried to throw it onto the train. It became part of their game. When I walked over to get my robe to exit, I innocently dragged it off by the neck, so that I had some of the dollars exiting with me, riding on the train, and yet I had not made any clear gesture that could be construed as meaning I wanted the money. The audiences went wild.

It was about this time that it was decided that I would have to find another song. The show had to go on. I could not hog the whole night. Even I could see the fairness of that. But find another song, a song lousy enough so that the audiences wouldn't call me back? That was like asking me to commit suicide as a comedian, if I was one.

---

## Incredible Vibrations

> Jazz will endure just as long as people hear it through their feet instead of their brains.
>
> —John Philip Sousa

We had many regular customers at the Bal. A man and his wife and an older lady came into the club quite often. They always asked for a certain table located next to the bandstand, practically touching it. They would take no other; they would wait for it to become available.

Everyone knows how a bandstand is set up. It is generally on three levels up from the dance floor: one or two steps up to elevate the leader, the saxophones, and the featured singers; another step up for the trombones and the trumpets; and a step higher for the tuba and the drums, which need plenty of room.

The older lady in this trio would always sit right next to the bandstand. For the whole time we were playing, she would rest her right hand on the carpeted bandstand beside her. When we were not playing, she would take her hand away. At first we were all curious.

Kay had long ago adopted the practice of "making the tables," which I had learned with Don Bestor. So from visiting various tables at the Bal, we soon learned that the lady with her hand on the bandstand was deaf. She could read lips well, and it was easy to talk with her. She told me one night: "I love your music, and I've learned how to enjoy life in spite of being deaf. You see, I pick up the vibrations of your music through the palm of my hand resting on the bandstand. I love coming here, love the rhythm of your band."

The man spoke up. "She hasn't always been deaf, only in recent years. We drive her up here to San Francisco quite often for dinner, and now she insists we only come here! Of course, to her, for a real dinner out, she has to be able to touch the bandstand." But they all raved about the food at the Bal—"Wonderful steaks," they said.

The deaf lady was an interesting person. One night she invited Kay, Janet, and me to visit her at her home. "I live at Carmel-by-the-Sea," she said. "We could sit on the beach, talk, and have some lunch." Kay said fine. So one day we drove down, and she showed us her home. She had colored lights all through the house. A green light flashed when someone rang the front doorbell; there was a yellow light for the back door and a red one for the phone. I wondered how she could talk on the phone. The answer was that she had a private listing, and if the red light flashed, she knew it would be family or friends checking on her. She could pick up the phone, tell them the news, and perhaps request something.

While we were having sandwiches, I nodded toward her piano and asked if she played it. She read my lips and said she used to, but no more. She had one of those old-fashioned music benches like we had at home—with sheet music spilling out from the inside, the seat hardly closing. Some of the music was in the form of big oversized sheets about twelve by sixteen inches. I knew music of that size was very old.

I asked if I could thumb through the music. She seemed glad to let me. Toward the bottom of the pile I came across a song called "Isch Gabibble." I picked it up idly, reading the cover page: "Written by George W. Meyer. Lyrics by Sam H. Lewis. 1908." (The very year I was born!) Inside were the words.

> I never care or worry . . . Isch Gabibble . . .
> Isch Gabibble
> I never tear or hurry . . . Isch Gabibble . . .
> Isch Gabibble

On paper the words did not promise much. But combined with gestures and a dumb face? Remember, I had been told to look for a song to replace the trapeze song, a song that would make the audiences *not want* to hear me! But my heart was not in the search.

Could I make this song a "small funny"? Just the "Isch Gabibble" was a bit funny. But those two words are hard to say. You can't get the *G* in "Gabibble" out without a full stop after "Isch." But maybe I could change the spelling.

I asked our hostess if it would be possible for me to borrow this piece of music. She held up her hands. "Oh, take it! Keep it! I don't want it. I had forgotten it was there." So we took it back to San Francisco with us. And that was the source of the Ish Kabibble song. I got permission to use it and decided to spell it "Ish Kabibble" to make it easier to say.

My style at the time was strictly deadpan—no expression at all. I would just get up there, do my thing, and sit down. I wore a tiny hat I had made out of cardboard and black paint. Under the spotlight, though, my throat was so dry that I could barely open my mouth to get the words out. Talk about butterflies. At times I was almost in a panic. If an audience is laughing with you, it's easy, so easy. But if they aren't, that's doing comedy the hard way! Still, I did get satisfaction out of playing my trumpet, so my nightly appearances on the stage were not a total loss.

After six months at the Bal, we moved down to Santa Monica

to the Del Mar Club for six months. The Del Mar was a private club at the time. Lewis Stone, one of the movie idols then, was a member, and he came there time and again to dance to our music. I was impressed. He was the first movie star I actually got to know.

Then we went back to the Bal for a few more months. I was still doing my Ish Kabibble song and still trying to get big laughs, but it was "no soap." Why did I keep trying? I don't know. I kept remembering the reaction to the trapeze act. I wanted that again.

---

## Bal Tabarin Shenanigans

> You heard of people who don't know nothin'? I don't even suspect nothin'.
>
> —Ish

B.D.J.—Before Disc Jockeys—there were song pluggers. The 1930s was their decade. They were hired by music publishers to push new songs. When a publisher put out a new song and wanted to have it played on the radio, which was the best way to make it popular and thus make money, the song pluggers would haunt the dance halls and the big bands.

There were perhaps two hundred of these men stationed across the United States. We got to know many of them, since they were generally stationed permanently in one city. Some of them were overly aggressive. They hung around entrances, hallways, and rehearsals. They tried to catch you at intermission to tell you about this song or that. In our case they were trying to see Kay. They pounced on us at the least expected time.

We had to learn to avoid them. We knew they were out there in the lobby or coffee shop or lying in wait for us somewhere. "Hey, get Kay Kyser for me, will you? I want to talk with him," they would say. We knew what they wanted, and we brushed them off. Kay had no time to see them all.

One particular song plugger was always hanging around the Bal. And he always wanted to get in free, even though he did not want to buy anything or order anything. He just wanted to see Kay. Frank Martinelli got tired of it and decided, "I'll fix this Joe so he'll never come back here."

The next time Joe showed up, Frank told him, "Gee, we've been looking for you. Golly! Come on in." He put his arm around Joe's shoulder. "You know, I guess you think Kay has been brushing you off. Well, I want to tell you what a nice guy he is. He told me the next time you came in, he wanted you to have a full-course dinner with us—on me, the manager, Kay, and the whole gang. It's our way to show you our appreciation for what you're trying to do—see that band leaders get good songs."

Joe was ecstatic. Frank ushered him to a prime table with a white tablecloth, white napkins, gleaming silver, the works. "Now you just sit down here, Joe. What would you like to drink before dinner?" Frank brought Joe his drink and said: "Now your dinner will be out shortly. It's going to be a surprise. We're not going to tell you what a great . . . Oh, well, I'll tell you 'cause I know you love it so. It's our spaghetti dinner!"

Joe was beaming. "Oh, Frank, your spaghetti is out of this world. I just appreciate this so much." He tucked his napkin under his chin and sat there with his knife in one hand and fork in the other. He was ready! And he was going to eat free!

In came the maître d' from the kitchen followed by waiters with a huge tray of silver service—the big dome with the handle on top—and they made a big to-do. We were all watching from the bandstand across the dance floor. We had ringside seats, but no idea what for. None of us knew what was coming. Kay, of course, had had nothing to do with it. It was all Frank's idea. The patrons noticed nothing. It was early, and there were few dancers.

The silver dome was put in front of Joe Plugger, and the waiters quickly loosened the silver top. Out jumped the most frantic cat you ever saw in your life. The hot spaghetti was dripping all over the cat, and the cat jumped all over Joe's face and lap and hair, making its getaway. Spaghetti flew in all directions, and Joe, at first scared to death, then realized that it was all a dastardly joke. He jumped up and stormed out of the place with spaghetti falling from him all the way to the street.

Many people who own cats will not like this story. But I am only telling it. I just saw what happened. I didn't participate.

Naturally Kay was always wanting new songs. If getting them from song pluggers was not the ideal answer, what was? Once when we were doing a movie, Kay needed about ten original songs, so he invited some real pros to play their new songs for him—people such as Jimmy McHugh and Hoagy Carmichael.

I remember that once on a sound stage—I believe it was at MGM—Kay had Jimmy and Hoagy come in, and they played some songs that were either not completed or had not been published yet. I especially recall that one day Hoagy played two or three songs, and none of us thought any of them would be hits. Of course, if any of us could have guessed in advance what was going to be a hit, we would all be millionaires. But life is not so simple. So we often picked the wrong songs.

That day Hoagy said: "Here's one I'm working on now, and I don't even have the words all written. But the first eight bars go like this . . ." He played a little snatch of a song, and the consensus was that it would never amount to anything. It turned out to be one of the greatest hits of all time—"Buttermilk Sky." And we turned it down! Later, after it became a hit all over the country, we recorded it, with Mike Douglas handling the lyrics. The only people who can decide whether a song is a hit are those known as "the public"—after you have recorded it and played it for them.

Years later, Kay did an about-face and gave a lot of attention to song pluggers. When we were in New York on radio, he set up a definite day each week, inviting all the song pluggers in New York City to come to our hall with their songs. He even served coffee. Kay and our arranger, George Duning, would sit and listen all day. I think Kay was among the first to adopt the policy of welcoming song pluggers on a weekly schedule.

## A Style of Our Own

Little spider on the wall,
You ain't got no hair at all.
You ain't got no comb to comb your hair.
What do you care? You ain't go no hair.

—Ish

We were playing at the El Miramar Hotel in Santa Monica. It was 1934. Band morale was at a new low. We did not seem to be getting anywhere toward becoming one of the big-name bands. Some nights after work we got in long discussions on why we were not "happening." Guy Lombardo was big time, and so were Wayne King, Hal Kemp, and others. What did they have that we did not have?

We decided the answer was a special style. They had an easily recognizable style of playing, and we did not. When you tuned them in on radio, no matter what song they were playing, you knew who it was. No announcer had to tell you. But we had no identifying style at all!

We had been through two or three years of ups and downs, when we sometimes had barely enough money to eat and travel and felt always on the verge of poverty, and it was getting to us. "Let's either stand up and be somebody or quit," we decided. We agreed to stay up all night every night, if necessary, rehearsing, in an all-out effort to create a style of our own. If we failed, we would break up the band and all go home.

Of course, we were still deep in the Great Depression, but who recognized that for what it was? As I said before, when you're in the middle of something like that, you don't realize that you are going through a phase. It is not until ten or fifteen years later, when, seen in perspective, the time is given a name, and then you say you experienced it.

We acquired a wire recorder. At 2 or 3 A.M. every night, we gathered in the empty dining room of the El Miramar. Each of us contributed ideas, and our arranger, George Duning, would orchestrate four bars of a song, which we would record on the wire recorder and then play back, listening, criticizing, and arguing. This went on night after night. We were looking for some distinctive ways of phrasing and voicing our arrangements.

Then something happened. Someone somehow hit on the idea of "singing song titles." We played a few bars of music at the start of some song, in which the vocalist would sing the words of the title, and then came a four-bar standard vamp of our theme song, "Thinking of You," during which Kay *talked* an introduction of the vocalist's name, timed exactly to fill up those four bars: "And now . . . presenting . . . Smilin' Bill Stoker . . ." And Kay's voice would have a smile in it!

We finally put together one complete arrangement of one song that we all agreed was distinctive and original, not copied from any other band. It was a style that might command some notice from the public, the critics, and the world of big bands. No sooner had we polished up this arrangement than we got an unexpected phone call to go to Chicago to start an engagement at the famous Blackhawk Restaurant.

Much as we welcomed the fantastic opportunity to follow Hal Kemp and his well-styled band into the celebrated Blackhawk, especially the once-in-a-lifetime opportunity to be heard several times a day on Radio Station WGN, we pleaded for more time to prepare our library in the new style. But the Blackhawk Restaurant wanted us immediately. Together with the WGN radio exposure, the Blackhawk had built many big bands, and it could be our doorway to success if we were prepared. Kay gave notice to the Miramar.

George worked night and day to arrange more songs, until our notice period was up. Then, once on the train, he locked himself into a bedroom of the Santa Fe Chief and arranged right up to the time the train pulled into the Chicago station. Going almost without sleep, he managed to complete fifteen songs in the new style—barely enough to fill the thirty-minute radio spot we faced opening day.

Opening day almost did not open. It came close to absolute catastrophe. Our first appearance and radio show was scheduled for 6 P.M. that opening night. At four that afternoon we were on the bandstand rehearsing a new girl singer, Maxine Gray, and the song was "I Saw Stars." We had "borrowed" her from Hal Kemp for a week or two until we could find a permanent singer.

Above our heads was suspended a canopy weighing two tons, full of neon tubing, lights, spotlights, and WGN microphones. Unknown to us, also up there, walking around on top of the canopy doing some special electrical wiring, was a 275-pound workman. His weight, plus the weight of the equipment, broke the slender chains holding the canopy, and down crashed more than two tons of electrical hodgepodge, smashing instruments and cutting heads, arms, and shoulders. Nobody was badly hurt, but we had only an hour and twenty minutes before the 6 P.M. broadcast and our first performance before the Chicago dining public.

We all "saw stars" for sure, and we also saw many of our valuable instruments damaged. Emergency word went out to music stores for substitute instruments. Doctors appeared and repaired cuts and bruises. Carpenters rushed in and tore away the remains of the canopy and nailed a large canvas on the wall to cover gaping holes. The customers began to arrive at their tables. At 6 P.M. we struck up our theme song, "Thinking of You," and we somehow got through our first big-time radio broadcast over WGN without the listening public being aware of the unbelievable problems of the previous two hours.

Soon after, Kay found his new girl singer—Ginny Simms. What an asset she was to our band! Kay hired her from Tom Gerun, co-owner of Bal Tabarin, who also had a band of his own in Chicago. Ginny was our big star for several years—until some time after the Kyser band went to Hollywood to make movies.

That first engagement at the Blackhawk lasted nineteen weeks—long enough for some smart guy to realize we had recording potential. One day he sent us down Michigan Avenue to make some records, among them the Ish Kabibble song.

I was excited and nervous. Was I actually singing on a record that might someday be played on radio? Since I did not have a trained voice, I figured I might as well just do it and let come out what would. After it was over, the engineer came out of his booth to ask, "What's the name of the vocalist on that side?" He meant me. I remember making sure he knew how to spell my real name. At that time I was not yet Ish Kabibble. I know that if I could find a copy of that old record today, the name Merwyn Bogue would be on it, listed as "vocalist," which, given all that has happened since, would seem strange.

## The Guy with the Haircut

An alarm clock will wake a man, but he has to get up by himself.

—Anonymous

When Janet and I were out on the road with the band in the early days, we did not have the dollars to stay in the plushier hotels or the inclination to stay in the other kind. In addition, there were practically no motels then. Occasionally, out on the edge of town you might spot a four-unit building with the new word *Motel* on a sign, but once you had, you rarely had the urge to sleep there. Many were crudely built, and most were drafty. In the winter, even though there was a pot-bellied stove burning all night, the occupant might shiver under the covers anyway, getting little or no sleep. Snow seeped through cracks, onto window sills, and under doors. In the summer you slept with flies and spiders.

What saved us were the tourist homes. There were plenty of them in every town. Residents erected signs in their front yard reading "TOURISTS WELCOME." It would be interesting to know how many families made it through the Great Depression by using such signs.

We paid anywhere from $1.50 to $2.50 per night for two. What we got in exchange was a clean, fresh-smelling room with photographs of Alice and Joe as babies, as children, on Graduation Day, and in wedding clothes; a recently added washbasin with the COLD running barely warm and the HOT running cold; and an old double bed that sloped toward the middle. Naturally we had to get dibs on the use of the bathroom with all members of the household.

How Janet and I used to yearn for luxury! We both liked "class" but got so little of it. No matter what our lodgings, we longed for greener pastures. Sometimes we stayed in nice places for short interludes. We would get a little cash, then spend it, get a little, then spend it.

Now we were booked into one of Chicago's finest restaurants, the Blackhawk—every band's dream! "We should be living in luxury," Janet told me and I told Janet. Yet we were living in an apartment on the near North Side that, for luxury, left a lot to be desired. But it was within what we could afford.

Right across the bridge in downtown Chicago was a renowned residence club called the Medina. It boasted such features as rubdowns, a swimming pool, steam rooms, and rooms with panoramic views of our beloved Chicago.

One day as I walked by the Medina Club, I had a sudden urge to live there. I went in to inquire about the rates. "Doesn't cost anything to ask," I thought. At that time we were paying thirty-five dollars a week for our dingy apartment. I walked up to the desk clerk and asked the rates for a nice room with twin beds and a view of the lake, and he said forty dollars. Well! It did not take me long to figure that if we were paying thirty-five dollars already, five dollars more would never break us. Surely we could think of *something* to give up!

Within two days we were moved in, enjoying the pool, the saunas, room service—the works. It was real class, and we had finally got smart and truly arrived. We now had a very prestigious address. Why hadn't we done it before? Everything was marvelous, and we relaxed and purred. What a place to come home to at night!

At month's end, our bill was slipped under our door. I noticed immediately that there had been a mistake. They had given me another man's bill. It totaled $1,425—$1,200 for the room, the rest for extras such as food, swims, and saunas. The man this bill was for must have money to burn.

So I sauntered—have you ever noticed that the rich always saunter?—down to the lobby desk and quietly handed the bill to the cashier, advising him of the error. He looked at it. "No, Mr. Bogue, this is correct. This is your statement," he said, and he handed it back to me.

"But . . . but . . ." I was stunned. I looked at the bill again so as to have something to do. "But . . . but I asked about your rates before I checked in. The clerk told me forty dollars a week. What about that?"

"You must have misunderstood, Mr. Bogue. Our rates are forty dollars per *day.*" Day? But that clerk had never said "day"! Then came the light, as I realized I had never *asked* him how much a day or week. I had been *thinking* week. In a regular hotel I would have walked in thinking how much a day. In an apartment or other living space I thought in terms of week or month.

I found myself staring at the man. I thanked him—what was I thanking him for?—and turned to walk away, though I could not manage to saunter. I told Janet. Our first reaction was to laugh for a solid hour. It was ridiculous! Where would we ever get $1,425?

Two days later we were back in our dingy apartment, minus our car, which we had sold in order to check out of the Medina Club. Armand Buissaret, our lead sax, bought the car, but we had to let it go for a song and not the kind you sing. What was the difference? we said. I couldn't sing anyway.

Without a car, we found much less to laugh at. But for that one month we were as good as rich, because we thought we were. What's so great about being rich? I would like to find out, just once.

Every night at the Blackhawk, I tried. Once every night I got up from my trumpet chair and ran down the steps to sing the Ish Kabibble song. The lyrics were no big deal, far from show-stopping.

I never care or worry . . . Ish
  Kabibble . . . Ish Kabbible
I never tear or hurry . . . Ish
  Kabibble . . . Ish Kabibble
When a friend says he's feelin' blue
When a friend says his room rent's due
Just tell him in a friendly way
    Get used to it
    Get used to it
When I owe people money . . . Ish
  Kabibble . . . Ish Kabibble
If they befriend or lend me . . . that's their
  lookout

They shouldn't yell and shout
I should worry if they steal my wife
And let a little pimple grow on my young life
Ish Kabibble . . . I should worry? No! Not
me!

There is a second chorus, which, luckily, I have partly forgotten.

Down the street from the Blackhawk, another band, I think it was Gus Arnheim's, was playing in a hotel ballroom. His trombone player doubled as a comedian and was getting big laughs with a song called "She Was Only a Bird in a Gilded Cage." Whenever I got time, I would sit in the audience and watch him with the greatest admiration. He was getting terrific laughs. He had an oversized handlebar moustache, big eyes, and funny facial expressions. Jerry Colonna was truly funny.

I asked him one night if he would come over to the Blackhawk and watch me and tell me what I was doing wrong. He came several times, watched, commented, and made suggestions. He told me many things. One was that it is not what you do or what song you sing so much as it is how you do it, and how you look when you do it. Funny clothes, he said, are only funny once—when you make your entrance on the stage. Clothes never get any funnier after the first look an audience gets at them.

"You gotta be funny from the neck up. Or forget it," he told me. He also said not to rely on funny song titles to make a funny performance. I had been trying to get laughs with a song called "Never Hit Your Grandma with a Shovel as She Just May Retort in Kind." I am not fooling—that was the title of a real song.

Jerry suggested that I try to think of something that would get people to call me the Man with the ———, the same way they called him the Man with the Moustache. "They didn't even know my name for a long time," he said. "But they'll learn your name after you get well-known, if you do."

Trying to learn from all that Jerry had told me, I got nowhere. So I decided to forget it. There would never be another song for me like "The Man on the Flying Trapeze."

We left the Blackhawk to do four months of one-nighters

through the Midwest, and one night—I think it was in Springfield, Illinois—I told myself, "This is my last night to go out there and sing 'Ish Kabibble.' After tonight, pfft." But in a final flash of defiance, something inside me said: "Why not have some fun with the boys in the band, at least? Why not do something that will surprise *them,* something for them to remember me by, something I did just before I quit?"

Pulling my comb from my pocket, I combed my hair straight down in front of my face. It was so long that it blocked my vision—I couldn't see where I was going. So I reached for a pair of scissors that were handy and cut my hair just above my eyes—not to get bangs but just so I could find my way onto the stage.

I walked on. The band was playing my usual entrance music, and when I turned to look back at them, they all broke up, and some quit playing. Even Kyser laughed! I started to sing the same song I had been doing for months, "Ish Kabibble," but the difference was that now the dancers stopped dancing, gathered close to the stage, and for the first time were really laughing! So I kept going, as Kyser whispered in my ear: "That's it, that's it. Never change that hairdo and we've got it made."

I never changed it, and I dropped my plans to quit the comedy. People began to call me the Guy with the Haircut. And the dancers called out: "Hey, Ish! Sing it again!" Thank you, Jerry Colonna!

---

## The Hoover Dam Derring-Do

What is the world worth to a man when his wife is a widow?

—Irish proverb

We had just finished a show for the workers at Hoover Dam in Nevada. The dam boss asked if some of us would like to go out and see how the work was coming along. Most of us were enthusiastic. He drove several of us to the bottom of the dam. It was night—about 2 A.M.—but the bright lights made it seem like day. "We are working this operation twenty-four hours a day because once you begin to pour concrete and it starts to run, you have to pour constantly or it will dry unevenly and crack," he told us.

The band members—Kay was with us—stood at the bottom of the huge wall, looking up in amazement. It was a lot of wall, and when you looked up, it was easy to see that you didn't amount to much.

The men were pouring concrete about six hundred feet in the air. We were looking at the equivalent of a building fifty to sixty stories high. The wall went straight up, but there was a slight angle away from you as the wall towered upward.

As we stood there, mouths gaping, a small wooden platform touched ground near us, and four workers stepped off. We said hello all around. They said, "Good show," and we said, "Fine dam you've got here" and stuff like that. I was glad I had come. It was exciting. The whole area was lighted up, and floodlights were playing all around. This was America at work. This was progress.

We asked the men how far up the little platform went. When one of them said, "Pretty close to the top now," I shivered. Boy! If a person had any fear of heights, he had better not get on that thing.

Little by little we were given details. The square wooden platform had four cables, one attached to each corner. Some distance above the platform, the four cables met and formed one single cable. The platform ran up and down the front of the dam on a little track, and the workmen were transported up and down the face of the dam on the platform. There were no railings. Each of the four men just stood on a square piece of wood in his own corner and hung on to his cable. I rubbed my palms together. They felt clammy.

I heard one of the workmen say, "When the platform gets beside the sliding ladder . . ." Now they were giving instructions on how to move from the rising platform to the sliding ladder. Well, all that had nothing to do with me. I stopped listening. I stepped a little away from the group, feeling remote from the whole discussion.

Then I realized that the workers thought that four of us from the band should take the ride up that wall. They thought it was an experience we would never forget. I looked around at Kay and the other guys. Who would the four be? Did any of them have the guts? I certainly did not.

Ordinarily I would be all for going along on most any adventure you might mention. But if there was one thing I was sure of that night, it was that I was not going to be one of any four to step onto that platform.

How I happened to be on it, a few seconds later, I will never understand. Was I dared? Did somebody give me a push? I have no idea. But four of us were on it, and the thing was starting up. My hands were grasping my cable so tight they hurt. I now remember nothing about how I got on that platform.

I turned for a second to look at the other guys. Kay was one of them, but I do not recall who the other two were. Nothing was said. There was no laughing or whooping it up. Turning back, my knees felt funny—tingly, as if they were turning to water.

As we rose in the air, I became increasingly scared. I had wet palms and was afraid to look down. The light did not seem as bright as it had on the ground. I shut my eyes and told myself, "Don't panic!" And I thought of Janet. I wondered what she would do without me.

Ages later, the platform shivered and stopped. I opened my eyes, and the first thing I saw was a huge wooden structure riding up and down in front of the dam and making a hell of a racket.

Well, the men back on the ground had pointed out the wooden structure and had said the platform would stop beside it. I felt a little better. Maybe things were going according to plan. The wooden structure looked about forty feet across and twenty feet high. It was moving up and down slowly over the face of the dam. The men had said it was on cables and that it smoothed and formed the concrete as the mixer poured.

Then I saw the sliding ladder. It was right beside us, attached to the wooden structure, moving up and down with it—fifteen or twenty inches up, fifteen or twenty inches down, up, down, up, down. Now I really was frantic. This meant, then, just what the man had said: "You are to get your left foot over onto one of the rungs of that ladder—take your pick—and get your left foot moving up and down with the ladder while your right foot stays on the platform, holding your main weight. Your left hand has to grasp some section of the ladder. Once your left foot and hand get to going it in a rhythmic motion, you are to choose your moment and switch your right foot onto the moving ladder."

Well, a person could almost lose his mind trying to get started to doing all that. It was like when one is learning to play golf. He stands there ready to swing and cannot get going, because of all the different things he has been told to do. The difference is that on a golf course you have your feet on the ground, even if you feel like a fool. Here there was nothing below us.

At first, none of the guys said a word. But after a few moments it seemed that everybody yelled above the noise at once: "Now is the time to make our move!"

"Who's going first?"

"You go!"

"I don't want to be last!"

Kay went first. I watched just what he did. He had guts. "I'll go next!" I yelled. Actually, I expected to die. What if my foot slipped on one of the rungs? It might be easier just to jump and get it over with, I thought. Poor Janet! What nonsensical talk was this? But what if I fainted? I felt a surge of dizziness.

I *had* to have what it took to do this, I told myself. I had to! I did what I had been told, did what Kay had done. He had climbed some distance up the ladder now, out of my way.

I grasped the moving ladder with my left hand, got it going, up and down. Then, keeping my eye on the rung I had picked as the one I would use, I carefully moved my left foot onto it, never looking down beyond the rung itself. Now my whole left side was riding up and down, but my weight was still on my right foot on the platform.

Up and down, up and down. Come on, Mern, I told myself, make the switch. OK, wait till it comes back up. Wait till the rung is flush with the platform. OK, now! And shifting my weight to my left foot, I grasped the ladder with my right hand. I was on! My hands were slippery with sweat, but I was on.

Now what? My knees almost buckled. I was not out of the woods yet. But now all I had to do was climb the ladder. I took a quick look up; it was about another 150 feet to the top. Kay was up there, still climbing. Climb a ladder? That was a cinch.

Dad had taught me to climb a ladder when I was four. But he never explained how to climb a moving ladder that jerks in space over the edge of a frighteningly high precipice as tall as a sixty-story building.

All right, Mern, up one rung, now another, I told myself. How was I going to get off this thing once I reached the top? Leap off? I worried about that as I climbed. But I found, once up there, that they had made that part easy. When you got on the top rung, the ladder sides extended way above you so you could hang onto them. You were flush with the top of the dam, and that was as far as the ladder went on its upward movement. So you just stepped off, while it was flush with the ground up there, onto a plank walk about ten feet wide. But the boards were wet and slippery, and that was not consoling. Yet we were up, and the ordeal was over.

Once we were all together up there, we thought there must be an elevator or some contraption over at the side of the dam next to the mountain that would take us down. We walked over to ask a couple of workmen.

"No, the only way to get down is to go down the same way you came up," one of them said, and they just kept on working. We stood gawking. I didn't see how I could do it. We stood looking off in the other direction, away from the drop, toward the mountains. Here we were, at the top of a 726-foot precipice, facing going back down, which seemed worse than coming up had been. We would have to make just the opposite of every move we had made coming up. (In a 1976 television broadcast of "Alistair Cooke's America," Cooke showed sections of the Hoover Dam and then nonchalantly entered an elevator and pushed a button, saying casually, "It's about sixty stories to the bottom." That was easy for him to say. But *we* didn't have an elevator!)

If you have ever stuck your foot over the side of a sixty-story skyscraper onto a moving ladder, you know how we felt at the start of our descent. But I don't want to think about it anymore.

## The Pittsburgh Flood and the High-Kicking Cornet

> I'd always recalled [Bogue] as primarily a dead-pan comedian. But apparently he also had a live lip.
>
> —George T. Simon, writer on Big Bands

"Here he comes, with the low-cut bangs and the high-kicking cornet!" Those were the words I often heard just before going onstage.

We were booked into the William Penn Hotel in Pittsburgh for a long stay that began in December, 1935. When that booking was nearly up, the waters of the Monongahela and the Allegheny rivers, which join at the Point to form the Ohio, were creeping through the downtown streets. Janet and I were staying at the Roosevelt Hotel in the lower part of downtown. When the water started to swamp the streets, it was a conversation piece. Then it grew into an inconvenience and finally was out of hand.

Rising fast, it flooded the first floor of the Roosevelt. We were rescued, going out of a second-floor window into a canoe. People grabbed motorboats, canoes, rafts, and anything else that would float, and headed for higher ground. Soon the whole of downtown Pittsburgh was underwater. The tips of trolleys were just visible out of the water; the streetcars were under.

Luckily the William Penn was on higher ground. We were paddled there, and the water was lapping at the hotel entrance. The place was almost like home to me, after the Don Bestor days. People fleeing other hotels were trying to get into the William Penn, and many were being turned away. But all our band members were given sleeping space because in the crisis the hotel wanted to provide music.

Several of us were offered space on the ninth floor. We let them know that this was not jim-dandy. The electricity was gone all over downtown, so the elevators were not working. By a strange coincidence both Ginny Simms and Janet were recuperating from recent appendectomies and thus would have to be *carried* to the ninth floor. We begged for other space, but rooms or makeshift accommodations on the first, second, and third floors were at a premium or gone. After watching the confusion in the lobby for a time, we took the ninth floor and were glad to get it.

The band played for two nights by candlelight. During this time it was rather like being on a sinking ship. Word spread that drinking water was running out. People drank bourbon, scotch, and other alcoholic beverages, including wine, from the bar until that, too, was gone. A drugstore across the street ran out of Poland Water. There was talk of epidemics. Downtown martial law was about to be declared because of looting. The more daring looters entered stores by pulling boats up to smashed windows.

We wondered if we could get out of town. A train was scheduled to leave across the Three-Point Railroad Bridge but was delayed because the tracks were underwater. In addition, authorities were worried that the bridge might be weakened by the swirling waters. They let it get further weakened by waiting another twenty-four hours. Then the railroad gave out word that anyone who wanted to go west could make reservations on a train leaving for Chicago the next day. It was made to order for us. Our next job was at the Trianon four days later. The band made reservations on this train.

After work that second night, I climbed the nine flights of steps to my bed. I was so thirsty I could not get to sleep. In a pocket I found a Lifesaver, which is almost as good as a swallow of water.

About 4 A.M. I got a sudden urge. I took my horn and in my pajamas made my way to the hotel roof. After standing for a few moments looking out over the water in the black of night, I raised my horn and played three choruses of "How Dry I Am" as loud as I could. It must have been heard all over downtown Pittsburgh and beyond. But no one ever said one word to me about it. I waited for days for someone in the band to mention it. They never did, the dogs. But I had the fun of doing it. Some of the guys must have heard it, but their fun was in not commenting.

The next morning we got on the train. It was way overloaded. It began to crawl across the Three-Point Bridge very carefully at about one mile an hour. In a time of crisis one's real character comes out. Some of the passengers turned out to be whiners;

others were comforters. Almost everyone was praying that the bridge would hold, some audibly. Some of us imagined the train was wobbling. It inched along, and the passengers grew paler. Nerves were stretched, including Janet's and Ginny's, with their appendix scars not healed.

When at last the train got across the bridge, it stopped, and the crew got off to check it over. Everyone cheered and whistled and applauded and thanked God and wanted to hug and kiss the engineer or somebody. It was a fairly dangerous thing for a train to do, now that I look back on it. I might have spent Eternity at the bottom of the waters where the Beautiful Ohio begins.

Radio Station WGN in Chicago specialized in putting on half-hour broadcasts from three famous dancing spots: the Trianon, the Aragon, and the Blackhawk Restaurant. One of the people I associate with the Trianon is Al Capone. Back then he was big stuff in Chicago and came to the Trianon often.

He had his own box near the ceiling, way up on the fourth floor. The Trianon had boxes for customers, like opera boxes, all around the dance floor—four tiers of them, where people could sit and watch the dancing. Watching dancers dance was big then. Capone sat high up so that no one could see him. No one but the band ever knew he was there. He would come three or four nights a week, with his bodyguards, and listen and watch.

He would send requests for Ginny, Sully, me or one of the others to sing a favorite of his. Afterward he would peek over the edge of the box, catch our eye, and salute us. We would watch for his salute. Of course, we all knew about Al Capone and his reputation, but to us he was a customer we aimed to please, so long as he chose to patronize the Trianon.

In the early months of 1937, Janet and I haunted baby shops; we were expecting our first child in April. On March 1, a month early, we had a boy! We were so dingbusted tickled and also relieved that it was over, and so proud of ourselves that we were a biological success. All day long I had spells of laughing and crying. All I could say was "Oh, boy!" I swung around the hospital room hitting imaginary punching bags.

Whenever Janet took a snooze, I went down the hall and sent telegrams or telephoned to family and friends. Two of the people I phoned were my sister, Gladys, and her husband, William J. Reilly, who was known as the Straight-Thinking Reilly because he wrote so many books on the subject. I got Janet on the line, and Bill told us: "You never know what life is all about until your first baby arrives and lets you know. After that, each new child you're lucky enough to have teaches you the same lesson. It's a tremendous feeling, Mern and Janet, and we know how it is. There's no happiness to equal it."

Janet and I shed a few happy tears. I was ten feet tall, and I guess Janet was touching the sky. We named the boy after me, but instantly we gave him the nickname Peter. They had him in a basketlike thing all covered with blankets, and they put a light bulb in there so that he could read and keep warm. But I told Janet: "He doesn't need an incubator. All he needs is some home cooking and about twenty years' time." And I was right, for he is a son to be proud of, with several college degrees, including a doctorate in education.

I found I had a brand new feeling for my own mother and father. I asked myself if this had been the way they felt about me when I was born. It couldn't be! How could they possibly love me as much as I loved our new little fellow? It was not until years later, when I became a grandfather and saw that my children did not realize that I loved them as much as they loved theirs that I saw this parade of life in its true perspective.

---

## Sold American

Mary had a little lamb.
His foot was full of soot.
And everywhere that Mary went,
His sooty footy put.

—Ish

We played the Trianon all the way through May and then did a weekly radio program for the Elgin Watch Company, still out of Chicago. So far, so good. I had not yet had to leave my new family.

Then we got a summer booking in Denver back at Lakeside Park, where we had played the previous summer. Pete was too young to travel when I went out there, but in July, when he was five months old, Janet and he traveled to Denver by train.

Ben Krasner owned Lakeside Park, and each year we returned he gave each of us a new uncirculated silver dollar from the Denver Mint, resting on cotton in a little box. I still have my two. Today the park is a shopping center, someone told me. I wish he hadn't told me. Some changes are not good changes and so are not worth hearing about or looking at.

Not long after we returned to the Blackhawk that fall, Kay hired Harry Babbitt as a singer. Harry was a terrific addition to our band. George Duning arranged numbers for Ginny and Harry, and they were an extremely popular duo for years.

WGN had a midnight to 1 A.M. program known as "The Midnight Flyers," which had a large audience in the Midwest. It had long been a tradition for all bands that played the Blackhawk to be heard on this program, and we wanted to think of something different to do for our broadcast. One hour is a long time to play constantly, because the brass men's lips give out or at least tire to the point of pain. So we tried to figure out what to do to give the band an occasional break.

At first we simply invited some of the other band leaders to drop by and chat or be interviewed by Kay on the air, which provided a brief rest. Ted Weems, for instance, would come and drop a few funnies like: "Kay, I felt so good last night, and I feel so bad this morning. It must have been that nasty old sleep I had." It may not seem funny today, but it was then. And you had to be there. Each band leader had his own charm. Today we might call it presence or charisma.

One night, as Ted Weems left the bandstand after a chat with Kay, Ted turned to me and said: "You got to come over to our place and hear my singer. He sounds exactly like Bing Crosby. A fella named Perry Como. I think you'll like him." I already knew about Perry Como because he lived in an apartment across the hall from Janet and me at the Drexel Arms. I went to hear him sing. Like him? There has to be a stronger word than that for audiences' responses to Perry.

Besides Ted Weems, many others made a habit of stopping by to be recognized and go on the air for a few minutes, band leaders such as Jan Garber, Wayne King, Shep Fields, and Hal Kemp. This had gone on for a few weeks when the musicians' union decreed that these people would have to be paid. Then for a while we kept a checkbook inside the piano near the strings, and I would write out checks for our guests during their appearances. Then the union made us stop it altogether, saying it was illegal.

We went back to filling the hour with music. But one day Kay called us together and suggested that we pick people from the audience to come onstage—three people on one side and three on the other—to be contestants in a little game. We would ask them a series of questions relating to music. Most of the questions would be in the form of the band playing eight bars of a song that the contestants would then attempt to identify. A winner was to be determined from each group of three, and then the two winners would vie in the final round, as we called it. The final winner would receive a modest prize such as a bottle of champagne.

The game was timed to fill exactly the one hour on the radio, and in between questions the band was featured or one of the singers did a specially arranged number. We thought it made a good show, but after a two-week tryout, Frank Schreiber at WGN decided to take it off the air. He and his colleagues thought such "quizzes" would be at best a flash in the pan. "And judging from last night," he added, "we don't think your show runs very smoothly." I could have told him why.

Naturally Kay had his questions numbered to correspond exactly with the eight-bar "questions" the band had rehearsed. I had volunteered to type the questions for Kay so that they would be easier to read. As I was typing, it occurred to me that it would improve the show if we slightly rearranged the order of questions, so I typed them in a different order from the one Kay had given me. Only I forgot to notify Kay and the band of the change.

So that night, when Kay would say to a contestant: "We will now play eight bars of a song, and we want you to name that song," and would turn to give the band a downbeat, out would come a wrong song or else complete silence, since the boys' sheets said to rest. That was probably the worst goof of my life.

Disgusted with myself, I went home that night and started packing my suitcase with the idea of leaving before I was fired.

But Kay, when I explained what I had done, not only forgave me; he convinced WGN the next day, when they brought it up, that if they would give us a few more weeks—the show aired only one night a week—we could markedly improve it. They relented and gave us a reprieve.

Kay hired a typist, Bess Clark, and she turned out to be a great friend and contributed much to our success with the show. From then on, Bess typed the questions and performed many other duties we had not dreamed we would ever have. No one in the band had any conception of how busy we were about to be. At last we were beginning to "happen."

The reaction from the WGN radio listening audience was fantastic. Mail came in by the bushel basket. Then Kay asked our listeners to send in questions, and if their questions were used, he mentioned their names on the show and sent them a diploma from the "Kollege of Musical Knowledge," personally autographed by himself! Instantly the mail started coming in by the truckload. Special arrangements had to be made with the post office for handling the flood of letters.

We dressed the stage to look like a college. Band wives went to work sewing costumes. Kay, with his cap and gown, became the Ol' Professor. I got out my flat black hat and glasses and became the Judge. The band dressed in striped college blazers. After about forty weeks, we knew we had a winner.

Between every dance set, the band pitched in and spent their entire break stuffing diplomas into tubes and addressing them for mailing. But no matter how fast we worked, we never caught up with the mail. We were always hopelessly behind.

We needed help, so we hired a young fellow, a jack-of-all-trades who had some knowledge of music. His name was Howard Miller. He did errands for us. I remember sending him to the post office with the diplomas. Later he became famous as a disc jockey in Chicago. Not only was he tremendously well liked, but without question he was the top earner of all disc jockeys in the Chicago area.

The volume of mail suggested that some company might be interested in sponsoring us as a national weekly radio show.

Hal Hackett of the Music Corporation of America went to New York to see what could be done. One of the sponsors he contacted was George Washington Hill of American Tobacco Company, who already was sponsoring the "Hit Parade," with Snookie Lanson and Dorothy Collins. We did not expect him to want a second radio show. Hal contacted many other potential sponsors.

One cold, rainy winter night about an hour before we were to do our show, I was standing in the lobby near the front entrance of the Blackhawk—my usual station to intercept bums trying to get in out of the cold and rain or wanting to "see Mr. Kyser." It was part of my job as band manager to sort out the panhandlers and questionable characters from the persons with good reasons to be there.

In came a bedraggled creature, soaked to the skin, who appeared to me to be just another "touch" wanting to see Kay. Claiming to have come all the way from New York City, he had a slightly different angle. I figured it was a likely story and tried to usher him right back out into the rainy streets of Chicago. Once I had wrestled him outside and told him to get lost, he handed me his card, which I made out in the dim light of the street.

AMERICAN TOBACCO COMPANY
GEORGE WASHINGTON HILL, PRESIDENT
NEW YORK CITY

Utterly appalled, I must have turned every shade from deep red to ghostly white. After many apologies, I ushered him in to see Kay. He seemed more amused than annoyed. He stayed to watch "The Kollege of Musical Knowledge" and said one thing when it was over: "How soon can you boys be in New York City to go on NBC for me and Lucky Strike cigarettes?"

Kay replied, "Just as soon as I can give Papa Roth, the owner, over there in the corner, two weeks' notice." So we were sold. It was July, 1938.

## Big Time

. . . busier than a Scotchman eating a paid dinner in a burning restaurant.

—Anonymous

On the train east, Kay told me, "Before we go on the air in New York, pick a name for yourself, because Ish Kabibble is not a name." By this time, I had adopted the philosophy of giving your employer more than you get, and so I had volunteered at every opportunity. I was now trumpet player, publicity man, transportation arranger, hotel reservations man, bookkeeper and paymaster, public address system installer in some cases, and, last and probably at that time least important, comedian. I was so busy I never got to think up a new name like Bob Hope or Red Skelton (a couple of guys were using those anyway). So before we knew it, we were doing our first broadcast, and it was too late for me to use any name but Ish Kabibble. Once a person was called a certain name over four hundred radio stations, if the public enjoyed what he did, he could not change it. The listeners would have said: "What happened to that guy you had last week? He was better than this one. Get the other guy back."

How did I accumulate all these duties? Actually, it was my own doing. It was never my nature to sit around. Shortly after joining Kay, I found that once daily rehearsal was over, there was nothing to do but wait to play the dance that night. I was ambitious and asked Kay if he had something I could do besides play trumpet. He needed someone, he said, to see to it that the bus was chartered, the correct uniforms on board, the hotel rooms reserved, and so forth. What he needed was a band manager. I could be that.

So I was that. But I was still sitting around some. I told Kay, "I know I haven't got a trained voice, but if I work up a couple of hillbilly songs, could I sing one once in a while?" Kay consented to that, too, and so I worked on it.

Then Kay said he needed a publicity man, and I volunteered. In San Francisco I used to go down to Herb Caen's office and light a cigar to appear sophisticated and blasé, and since he had his feet up on his desk, I would put mine there, too, and we would talk. I gave him material to print about Kay, stuff I knew Kay would like known. Today Herb still has a syndicated column; I see it in the Honolulu paper.

Then after Earl Bailey, our booking agent, left us to go with MCA in Beverly Hills, we needed someone to pay the band boys, and I volunteered. I handled the books and the money for many years, until it was coming in faster than I knew how to handle it. So Kay hired a professional accountant, Burr Blair, and I turned it over to him. I carried the loudspeaker equipment in my car and in small towns installed it before the dance started. When we traveled by bus, I was the one who jumped out first, ran into the hotel, and bargained for twenty rooms, haggling over the price. Eventually, as our success grew, I chartered Pullman cars and airplanes. I still played trumpet, did the comedy, and "checked the gate" when we played percentage dates. I kept one eye on the music I was playing, the other eye on the promoter at the front gate.

I did those things because I wanted to be busy; I got no extra salary for any of them. I did them to help Kay. Not until toward the end of the Lucky Strike days did I ask for more money.

Once we were in New York, the band members found places to live. Janet and I got a place in Forest Hills. Rehearsals started at NBC in preparation for the first broadcast. George Washington Hill was present at most rehearsals. He contributed suggestions. We did not like some of them, but some were great.

The one suggestion we particularly did not care for was that we stop playing Kay's uniquely styled endings to songs. He said: "Take those off. Just play a big, loud chord at the end. That way all our home listeners will know the song is over and the time has come to mentally applaud." We did not want to do it, because those endings were one of Kay's trademarks. But slowly we converted to big, loud chords. After all, Mr. Hill was paying the freight.

After having heard Speed Riggs and Basil Ruysdahl do the commercials on the "Hit Parade," which Mr. Hill also sponsored on a different day of the week, we found it thrilling to have them come over to our program and do the same ones. There was a famous commercial with an auctioneer that ended with the phrase "Sold American." At first Speed Riggs did it all. Later, Speed just did the chant, and Basil Ruysdahl followed with the pitch. Speed Riggs was probably the highest-paid person in the world given the hours he worked. He would do the chant three times, grab his trench coat, and go home.

We began to experience the "big time." We had the great Ben Grauer for an announcer. It was a kick to realize we were being heard all over the nation each week. The long hours of rehearsals, the hundreds of one-night stands, the headaches, the reversals—they were all paying off now.

Every broadcast day, after rehearsal and before show time, we took a break. One of the nice things about this period was that, when we returned to our chairs after the break, there would always be a carton of Lucky Strikes on our chairs with a small card that read "Compliments of Mr. Hill." It was a much-appreciated gesture.

But there always has to be a bad apple in any barrel. One or two of the boys did not smoke Lucky Strikes. They would go into the drugstore in the NBC building on the street level and trade them in for their own brand. One day Mr. Hill happened to be enjoying a chocolate soda in the drugstore and witnessed one of these transactions. From that day on, the chairs were noticeably empty on broadcast day. It only took one or two jerks to kill it for the rest of us.

Since the radio show only took one day a week, we took other jobs. At one point we were appearing daily on the roof of the Pennsylvania Hotel, making records almost every day, and at the same time doing seven shows a day at the Roxy Theater. For a while we were actually running so fast between places that I had to order ten Yellow Cabs to be waiting at stage doors to whisk us and our instruments to the next place. And at lunch- and dinnertime, trays of food would be waiting in the cabs so that we could eat on the way to where it was we were going.

## The Three Little Fishies Story

Some fish are fat and some fish are thin;
Some fish are long and some fish are short;
They can't walk and they can't talk,
But they can stay under water longer than
anybody.

—Ish

Our records were becoming hits—some of them, anyway. About one out of fifty was a hit, and that was considered a good average. It was, for me, a new experience to be out somewhere and hear one of our songs, "The Three Little Fishies," for example, played on a radio show and to hear my voice along with the others.

There is a story about "The Three Little Fishies" that is not generally known. As far as I know, it has never been told in print. It should be told; the girl who wrote the song should have more recognition than she ever got. I wish I could tell you her name, but I do not know it. Yet she and I are probably the only two people who know the song's earliest history.

The band had done some 78 rpm recordings for Columbia Records in New York. We had done seven sides and knew we were to do an eighth. We were in Philadelphia working in the Earl Theater when Columbia sent word they wanted the eighth side pronto. Kay said: "We have to go upstairs and do that eighth side. Anybody got any ideas?"

Four or five years before that, we had played for a dance at the University of Virginia. At such events it often happens that one or more would-be songwriters approach members of the band with some scrawled notes and ask, "Can you do something with this song of mine and make me a millionaire?" They usually laugh as they say it, and dance past as though they are kidding. But they're not. They're hoping.

That night at the University of Virginia, a girl came over to me—I happened to be closest—and asked if I would consider looking at her song to see if we could do anything with it. I smiled and took it—we were used to such requests—and since I never looked them over right away, I did not notice that her name was not on the paper. We were busy packing up to get on the road to our next place, and I just tossed it in my suitcase. From then on in every hotel, after I took my clothes out of my suitcase, that song would be lying there, in the bottom of it. The song collected dust, dirt, and lint, and it stayed there for four years.

One night I ran across Saxy Dowell, who was a singer and saxophone player for Hal Kemp. He sang sort of like Sully Mason. They were called scat singers. Saxy and I were talking about songs, and he asked me to let him know if I ever ran across any songs suitable for him. By this time I had looked at the song and knew that the girl had not even put her name on it. But I gave it to Saxy. "Here, I've been carrying this around for four years," I said, and I told him about the girl at the University of Virginia dance. "She didn't even put her name on it or give me her name. Why don't you look at it and see what you can do?" I don't know why I had never given the song to Sully, who was one of my closest friends. But it just happened that I was talking with Saxy about the availability of songs.

Soon Hal Kemp had a record out called "The Three Little Fishies in the Itty Bitty Poo," but it was not a hit. It was a straight musical thing, and Saxy did the singing, but it missed out. Somewhat later I ran into Saxy. He gave the song back to me, and I don't know how much longer I carried it around.

Finally there came that day in the Earl Theater when Kay asked for ideas for that eighth side. I said: "I've got this tune called 'The Three Little Fishies.' I gave it to Saxy Dowell, and Hal Kemp recorded it but nothing happened. Maybe we can give it a little different interpretation and do something with it." And I quickly told Kay the rest of the background surrounding the song.

Kay and George looked at it. "Yeah, maybe we can sketch out something," they decided. So they did, and we recorded it, just the way they dreamed it up right there. It was all done in a great hurry, with a lot of improvisation and without much planning or rehearsing. But in terms of number of sales, it was probably the greatest tune that our band ever had:

Down in the meadow in the itty bitty poo
Swam the three little fishies and the mama fishie too.
Swim, said the mama fishie, swim if you can
And they swam and they swam all over the dam.

And I came in with my "dittem dottem whattem chu" or a "riddle diddle dazzle brrrp" or a "skiddle-de-did," and that was the way the song came out.

But during the time when Saxy had the song, he had had to get it published in order to convert it to sheet music. He needed a composer's name for the song, and he wound up putting down his own—not in any sense to claim he had written it, but just to get it published.

Then along came the girl from the University of Virginia with an attorney. I did not know anything about this part of the story until long after it happened. Saxy never told me about it. But the dispute was settled in the courts. The courts ruled that Saxy should leave his name on the song for posterity and could enjoy its monetary fruits from then on, but that the girl was to have a cash settlement amounting to all the royalties the song had earned to that point, which were considerable. The girl and Saxy settled for that. Both of them found the settlement generally satisfactory, though Saxy felt that the girl's name should have been put on the song. It was not until much later that I learned of the settlement, and by then Saxy was dead. And I still do not know the girl's name!

In 1939 when we were asked by RKO to go to Hollywood to make a full-length movie featuring the band, there was much kidding around, naturally, about our being big movie stars and all that. When we arrived and started meeting some of the stars, it was like a dream to me that we were really there and I was part of it. This was *me,* from Erie, Pennsylvania, shaking hands with Lewis Stone again, being in the movies with Lucille Ball and later with Joan Crawford and John Barrymore, and knowing Bob Hope and Red Skelton. You have to be careful in such situations—when you're meeting new stars every day—that you don't get overly impressed with yourself.

When we left New York to do the first movie, *That's Right, You're Wrong,* I walked into a typewriter store on 42nd Street just east of Fifth Avenue and made arrangements for them to ship my typewriter out. After the clerk explained how carefully they would pack it, I was still apprehensive, and so he took me in the back room and showed me the packing material he would use and the way he would crate it. He kept reassuring me, and finally I left feeling satisfied.

Some months after that, when I was in New York again, I returned to the store and looked for the clerk I had talked with before. When he asked what he could do for me, I launched into a tirade: "I hope you remember me. I was in here about six months ago and wanted my typewriter shipped to Hollywood, and you promised you could send it safely. You said you knew how to ship typewriters." He looked increasingly nervous. "You even claimed that was your business. I believed you and I let you ship it. Why, you even took me in the back room and showed me exactly how you would crate it with all your great packing material."

"Yes, I remember that, but . . ."

"Oh, you can say what you want, but you promised it would get there OK. You promised. And you want to know something? I just stopped in to tell you it did. It got there OK! Thanks!" And I turned and walked out of that shop without once looking back. One of the hardest things I ever did in my life was to keep from turning around to see the expression on his face.

---

## Skulduggery

He is winding up the watch of his wit.
By and by it will strike.

—William Shakespeare

Webster defines *practical joke* as "a joke whose humor stems from the tricking or abuse of an individual placed somehow at a disadvantage." Although I cannot speak for other bands, the classic pastime of our band was the practical joke. That was because we had a true joker in our midst—Lyman Gandee. How he loved to play one! He was our piano player and was so good that he did not have to think about what he was doing. His fingers did the playing, and he had plenty of time while they skipped over the keys to dream and plan his skulduggeries.

I never considered myself a natural-born practical joker, like Lyman, though I like fun and learned to defend myself. You can't go out on one-nighters day after day after day with the same guys, travel with them on buses, work with them, eat with them, sleep in their general vicinity, and wait around with them, without manufacturing a little fun and a few dirty tricks.

Lyman joined Kay in 1932, a year after I did, and he left shortly before Kay broke up the band the first time, about 1946 or 1947. So he had about fifteen years to establish himself as the band's self-appointed Master of Practical Jokes, and the day finally came when it was "the whole band against Lyman." By then he had pulled some lulus, with band members as the butts. He swears today, though, that he never played a practical joke on anyone he did not like. I believe that.

Lyman particularly liked one routine in which he had me play a drooling idiot. I can't say that I liked it, but he did. He tried it whenever conditions were right. He could somehow talk me into it by promising he would never ask me again. "Just one more time, Ish. Come on!" he would say.

The gag started when we were playing a St. Louis country club in the mid-1930s. Lyman and I rode back and forth to work together in his car. Every night on our way home, we stopped in a small "one-arm restaurant," as it was called back then, for a bite to eat. It was a one-man operation, in which the owner took your order, cooked it, served it, and took your money on your way out. On our first night there, Lyman saw the setup.

He whispered to me, "Put your teeth in and pretend you can't talk and we'll have some fun with this guy." I started to protest, but he already had me by the hand and was pulling me toward a booth. I had a set of ugly-looking false teeth that I sometimes used in my act to make me look extra stupid. Lyman knew I carried them in my pocket. I did not want to put them in here, but he kept nudging me with his elbow. So I slipped the teeth in. Anything for a little fun for one night, I thought.

Lyman ordered for us, pointing to me and explaining, "He can't talk." It was not easy to eat my cornflakes through those protruding teeth. The milk kept running down my chin, delighting Lyman and embarrassing me. But so what?

It did not occur to me that first night that I was ever to repeat this performance—on the next night, for instance, and the next, and it soon seemed, so on forever. But Lyman was driving, and I had to eat where he did or wait in the car.

Soon the owner was watching for us and being especially kind to me, wanting us to know that he understood and sympathized. After a while I felt terrible. I don't know why we dragged it on so long, but it became a regular nightly act for several weeks. I wanted to quit and tell the guy or else never go back. But Lyman kept saying: "Wait, Ish! Wait!"

Finally it was our last night in town. This time, as we left the restaurant, I took the check to the cash register for the first time. When the owner came to take the money, I looked him straight in the eye, took the teeth out, said clearly, "How much do we owe you?"

He did a very long take; I thought it would never end. We could almost see his mind turning over. I thought he would laugh and was ready to laugh with him, but he got mad. Slowly he reached behind him and took a fifteen-inch cheese knife from a shelf and started after us. He chased us three blocks but could not catch us.

At the Miramar Hotel in Santa Monica, Lyman once slipped a big hunk of limburger cheese down through the S-shaped holes in Butch Shonka's fiddle during an intermission when we were all gathered outside in the garden. Whenever a violinist tucks his fiddle under his chin and adjusts it to get comfortable, his nose, of course, is directly over the S-shaped holes. No one, unless it was Kay, knew why we had a fiddle in the band. There was no music written for Butch, but now and then he picked up his fiddle and played the melody along with us.

Lyman was a clever one. In the Miramar garden he arranged things so that Butch was the last to go back to the bandstand, and somehow Butch got locked outside. The only way Butch could get back to the bandstand was to run like hell down a long block and around through the front door of the hotel. Butch was by no means fleet of foot. So he was late, and Kay did not like it when anyone was late. Butch got a bawling out, though Kay knew how to do this quietly, so that the audience would not notice. Nevertheless the offender knew exactly where he stood, and it was not on firm ground.

We were well into the first chorus of the first dance tune by the time Butch slipped onto the bandstand. He wasted no time grabbing his fiddle and tucking it neatly under his chin to perform his part of the melody. By then, the rest of us had sniffed the atmosphere and recognized Lyman's touch. So we were all watching out of the corners of our eyes when Butch, after a whiff or two, tore the violin away from his throat and stared at it in astonishment, wondering what had happened.

But we all suffered from this joke, since we had to breathe limburger the entire rest of the evening. Sure, Lyman had to smell it, too. But he liked limburger! Mostly it was Butch who suffered. He had to pay a pretty penny the next day at a violin maker's shop to have his fiddle fumigated.

Lyman's *pièce de résistance* was a joke he pulled on Harry Babbitt. When "The Kollege of Musical Knowledge" was at the peak of its popularity, we were booked into the Roxy Theater in New York. At that time the policy of the Roxy was to have a line of some forty-eight dancing girls working under long-term contracts that required them to appear each week in every stage production. When our show went into the Roxy, we did not need the girls, since it was a game show that used only ourselves and members of the audience. But their contract dictated that they must be paid each and every week as long as they were on the payroll, and so the problem was to find something to do with the forty-eight dancers during the week we were there.

It was decided that the girls would be used in the background in a dim light to enhance the ballads that Harry Babbitt would sing. The result was many different formations and movements behind Harry as he sang, one of which had twenty-four girls on one side of the stage and twenty-four on the other, all dancing toward Harry from the rear in an arrow formation, passing directly behind him. He was dressed in an all-white formal long-tailed cutaway. A small pinpoint of white spotlight beamed on him from head to toe. Naturally, all eyes were focused on Harry during his numbers.

The routine called for the first girl in one of the lines of twenty-four to tippy-toe up to Harry and swan-dance for a moment practically at his left ear. One night, as she reached him, she whispered softly into his ear the words Lyman had told her to say: "Your fly is open."

Harry believed it, figuring that with his cutaway coat he was really on display full bolt in front of that packed house. He never lost control of his song, but he died a few times until he could make his exit and check. He found himself impeccably groomed, as always. And then, of course, he knew who was responsible.

The main thing about Lyman's jokes was that the victim never tumbled until it was all over. It never seemed to dawn on you that "This is just like one of Lyman's jokes." He seemed to like you so much!

Lyman must have liked Harry a lot, but everybody liked Harry. He and I spent a lot of time together. We shared the same background. When he joined the band, we discovered that we were both members of DeMolay. In fact we were the only DeMolays in the band. That alone made us special friends. Once when we were playing Kansas City, the man who founded DeMolay, Frank S. Land, sent for Harry and me and initiated us into DeMolay's Legion of Honor. We are both very proud of that honor.

Many were the pranks that Lyman played, and to get back at him was always a challenge. After the band had been in Hollywood making movies for a while, we all had small bank accounts. Lyman bought a pedigreed French dog and decided he would put it out at stud, charging "a big fee," he said, "to make lots of money."

An especially important rehearsal was coming up, and Kay laid down the law that anyone who was late for this 1 P.M. rehearsal at NBC Hollywood the next day would probably be fired. "So everybody be here on time!" he concluded.

The next day about 11 A.M. Janet, my wife, called Lyman on the phone, disguising her voice. Affecting a French accent, she called herself Madame Fifi and asked if she could hire the services of his French poodle to mate with her "dahling poochie."

She had made inquiries at the place where he had bought his doggie, and "Je suis enchantée" with the report, she said. "À tout prix," she assured Lyman. Money was no object.

Lyman was quick to accept and named an exorbitant fee, which Madame Fifi accepted. But she was very "busee," and the only time she could meet him to give her Poochie to him was that day on her way to the airport. She was off to New York and wanted to settle "thees thing today." She suggested meeting at 1:30. Lyman explained that he had an important rehearsal at one o'clock and could not meet her at 1:30, since it would make him late for work. Madame Fifi then told him to forget it, that she would find another owner—at the kennel, perhaps.

Lyman agonized, not wanting to miss this chance. He finally agreed to meet her at 1:30 sharp, and they arranged a meeting place. He said, "I'll have to bring someone along to take the dog home."

Sure enough, at 1 P.M. the whole band except for Lyman was at rehearsal. I was the only one in the whole room who knew where he was—at Sunset and Vine waiting for Madame Fifi, who had no intention of showing up.

At around 1:45 Lyman appeared, red-faced and angry, but he would not tell the truth about why he was late. He said he had car trouble. Kay, of course, did not fire Lyman. He may even have suspected that Lyman had been "had."

It was not until one day about fifteen years later, when I happened to be talking on the phone to Lyman about something, that I said: "Oh, incidentally, there's an old friend of yours here who wants to say hello to you." Janet took the phone and said: "Hello, Meester Gawndee. Thees is Madame Fifi . . ."

I always liked Lyman. I would never play a trick on anyone I did not like.

---

## Hollywood Doings

The crisis of yesterday is the joke of tomorrow.

—H. G. Wells

When we went to Hollywood to make our first movie, Janet and I rented apartments by the month. Our first apartment was located on Durant Drive in Beverly Hills. Skitch Henderson lived near us with his little black dog. Our first landlady was a Mrs. Hooker. Our next two landladies were Mrs. Ketchum and Mrs. Grabbengetter.

The first movie featuring Kay Kyser and His Band was *That's Right, You're Wrong,* directed by David Butler. Lucille Ball—a starlet just beginning her career—was in that picture. Butler directed several Kyser movies, but it was during the making of the first one that Janet and I really got to know him. We were invited on several occasions to his home at Malibu.

In the fall of 1939, Janet and I paid a visit to a baby doctor recommended to us, Dr. Irving Ress. A lot of movie people were patients of his. Besides being your doctor, Dr. Ress was also your friend. He was one of the most generous persons I have ever known. He gave big dinner parties for his patients, sometimes attended by thirty or forty people, and he always gave wonderful gifts.

Janet and I learned to love this man. Later, during the war, when certain items were scarce because of rationing, our doorbell sometimes rang in the middle of the night, and we would get to the door just in time to see Dr. Ress's Cadillac taking off down the street. On our patio or doorstep would be a box of sugar or some butter or bacon or other rationed item. It seemed to us that all his free time must be given to doing thoughtful things for his patients. And he was a busy and famous man. At one time he was head of B'nai B'rith. He was also elected to the National Academy of Surgeons.

Not long after we moved to California, Dr. Ress had to tell Janet that if she wanted to hang onto the baby she was carrying—our second—she would have to stay in bed for the remaining seven months of her pregnancy. Did she want this baby bad enough to do that? he asked her. Yes, she told him, she did.

It was during this trying time for her that David Butler did a nice thing. Our movie was out, and of course, Janet could not go see it. So David brought the movie to her. He brought his whole camera and sound equipment to our apartment. I was out on the road, but Janet and her mother, Effie Meade, invited some friends and neighbors, and David showed *That's Right, You're Wrong* on the ceiling of our bedroom!

Dennis O'Keefe, Hedda Hopper, Louella Parsons, and other movie and radio columnists were in that picture. Meeting them, on top of getting to know David Butler, was pretty hot stuff for a kid with roots in a barn in the middle of Erie, Pennsylvania, with no relatives or relatives' relatives to give him a boost in show business.

David used to sit and tell me stories about his life as a director. I liked one especially, I suppose because it had to do with a trumpeter.

"It was back in the days of silent pictures," David recalled. "We were going to shoot a scene from about a mile away, and the cameras were high on a hill." It was a picture for Fox Studios, and the mock-up of an old castle had been built—just the facade and a few rooms, so that they could shoot some interior shots. At the end the whole castle was to be dynamited, with the cameras rolling.

Building the set had cost the studio a million dollars. It was constructed out in a field at Fox Studios in Beverly Hills. As time neared to shoot the final scene, two days were spent planting the dynamite charges. Men were stationed on twenty-four-hour guard to watch the box that would set off the charge. Nobody was to touch the box ahead of time.

"I told the guard," said Dave, "that we had to have some signal worked out for when he was to blow it. The distance was too far to see a hand signal. So I hired a cornet player from the musicians' union, and I told the guard, 'When you hear this fellow do the bugle call on his cornet—you know, de dat de de dat—that's your signal to blow it up.'"

The explosion was set for 8 A.M. At 7:30 the actors were already there, the cameras were arriving, and the cornetist showed up. Dave told him, "Just play the old bugle call—you know, de dat de de dat." The musician said, "Fine," and went over and took his horn out of his case. Dave called to him: "Just hang on, now. It'll be a few minutes yet. I'll wave to you when you're to blow."

The cornetist said OK and walked a little farther away, fingering his valves. A brass musician always likes to warm up his lip, so he was doodling around. For some reason Dave did not like the way the kid was acting. He hoped the young fellow remembered how the bugle call went.

"It must have been on an impulse," Dave recalled. "Or maybe the kid decided to loosen up his lip and, well, practice. I think he thought he'd practice quietly—that's how it must have been. But anyway—God knows why—he suddenly bent back and out came de dat de de dat. . . . Do I need to tell you what happened? The blaster down below thought it was the signal, and he blew up the castle. A million dollars went up in smoke and not a camera was rolling!"

Slowly Dave turned toward the trumpet player, and the kid saw Dave start for him. The poor guy never even bothered to put his horn back in his case. He just left the case there and ran. Dave chased him down the hill and out of sight. "Nobody," said Dave, "ever saw him around Los Angeles again."

By 1940 everything was happening at once. In April our little Pamela was born, and now we had a boy and a precious little girl. I had lots of fun with them, but it had to be snatched between bookings. We were still doing the Lucky Strike program, either from New York or Hollywood. Sometimes Janet could go, sometimes not. We did a lot of one-night stands and assorted appearances, put together by our manager Lyle Thayer. We would have been lost without Lyle's services during those hectic days. He was a genius, booking us into such places as Catalina Island off the coast near Los Angeles, the Pennsylvania Hotel and the Waldorf in New York, the William Penn Hotel in Pittsburgh, and Frank Daley's Meadowbrook near New York. Back in Hollywood, we made *You'll Find Out* for RKO.

In 1941, Kay and the Band did *Playmates* for RKO, with David Butler again directing. It was a haunted-house horror movie with Bela Lugosi, Boris Karloff, Peter Lorre, and, among others, Ish Kabibble. One scene called for me to be in bed sleeping when I heard a noise in the dark. I was to lean out of bed, look at the heating grate, and see a hand coming through it holding a knife, the sight of which would make my bangs stand straight up in the air. Then I was to fall on the floor in a faint.

What a great to-do it took to make my hair stand up. Someone brought a big contraption from the University of California that looked like an upright piano with a glass front through which you could see all sorts of copper disks whirling around in circles and making an unholy racket. The purpose of this machine was to create an electrical suction. Somebody washed and dried my hair till it was filled with static electricity. Then they sat me down and lowered a huge copper plate to a point about four inches above my bangs but out of camera range. They cranked up the machine, got the wheels going at full speed, and then turned a switch that threw the electricity into the copper plate over my head. My hair was now supposed to stand on end.

Instead, a spark flew out from the disk to my damp scalp and *I* stood on end! Out I went as if I had been hit with a brick.

Also, to faint dead away on the floor might be considered easy and amusing by some, but to me it got monotonous. After doing it four times over a period of a few hours, I rebelled. I had had enough lumps for one day, I told them.

Next day we started again. They finally got the scene. And I got a clean head—clean and sore. They must have washed my hair six or seven times in two days.

In April, 1941, the radio show "Hedda Hopper's Hollywood" was one year old. Hedda wanted some publicity to celebrate her first successful year, so she hired Paul Moser, our publicity man, to find a one-year-old baby girl who would model some of Hedda's ridiculous hats, which were her trademark. Paul remembered our daughter Pamela, who had just had her first birthday. Hedda brought her hats and her cameraman to our house and made it a big day for the Bogues.

In October little Janet was born, and we learned all over again that each child is a separate bundle of love. Now we had three little fishies in our itty bitty poo, and that was all the Mama Fishie was supposed to have.

But there is something to be said for large families. My mother was the seventh child in her family, my father the eighth in his. So if it were not for large families, I would not be here.

Ish at four years of age

Ish's father at four

Emaline Orpha Parsons Bogue, Ish's mother, in about 1900

Ish's father, Martin H. Bogue, and his stepmother, Mabel Mong Bogue

Ish's wife, Janet Meade Bogue, in 1934

Ish and his children—Pete, Pamela, and Janet—in 1946

The Kay Kyser Band at the Bellerive Hotel in Kansas City in 1932. *Front row, left to right:* John White, Al Schmidt, Sully Mason, Mary Wine, Kay Kyser, Benny Cash, Ray Michaels, Ish Kabibble. *Back row, left to right:* Lyman Gandee, Jack Barrow, Ray Grumney, Pete Fleming, Art Walters.
*Courtesy Georgia Carroll Kyser*

Kay Kyser as the Professor of "The Kollege of Musical Knowledge"
*Courtesy Georgia Carroll Kyser*

Ish on opening night at the Blackhawk Restaurant in Chicago in 1937

Sully Mason
*Courtesy Georgia Carroll Kyser*

Ginny Simms
*Courtesy Ginny Simms*

Georgia Carroll Kyser
*Courtesy Georgia Carroll Kyser*

George Duning

Harry Babbitt
*Courtesy Harry Babbitt*

The Kay Kyser Band at the Steel Pier in Atlantic City in 1940
*Courtesy Georgia Carroll Kyser*

John Barrymore, Kay Kyser, and Ish, during the filming of the movie *Playmates* in 1944

*Photo by John Miehle, RKO Pictures, Inc. Courtesy Georgia Carroll Kyser*

Between movies the band appeared many times at the Casino on Catalina Island. *Front row, left to right:* Eddie Shea, Max Williams, Lloyd Snow, Ish Kabibble, Armand Buisseret, Sully Mason, Harry ("Breezie") Thomas. *Back row, left to right:* Lyman Gandee, Herman Gunkler, Jack Martin, Kay Kyser, Ginny Simms, Harry Babbitt, Pokey Carriere, Bobby Guy.
*Courtesy Georgia Carroll Kyser*

General Douglas MacArthur

In 1970 Merv Griffin did a television special featuring band leaders and personalities from the Big Band Days. That's Merv kneeling in front. *First row, left to right:* Les Brown, Connie Raines, Helen Forrest, Charlie Barnet, Xavier Cugat. *Back row, left to right:* Vaughn Monroe, Lawrence Welk, Ish Kabibble, Horace Heidt, Freddy Martin, Stan Kenton.
*Courtesy Merv Griffin Enterprises*

Ish in the early 1950s

Ish and Janet at their fiftieth wedding anniversary celebration on Maui

# 3

## ISH IN WORLD WAR II

## Lucky Strike Green

. . . about as influential as the *p* in pneumonia.
—Anonymous

Then came Pearl Harbor. Every man under thirty-eight registered for the draft. Indignation flared at the Axis powers, and the people of this country threw away their political whatevers, and the spirit was "Let's cooperate and win this war."

We learned what rationing was. The consumption of food, gasoline, and heating oil was strictly regulated. Ration books were issued to every person in the country, no matter what age they were—babies and all. But no family had enough ration stamps to fill its needs. Nobody had enough heating oil to last until the next "allowance," even though thermostats were kept at sixty-five and sometimes below. Men went to army camps and navy and marine bases. Women who had never worked outside the home got up at the first crack of dawn—even on Christmas Day—and went to work at 7 A.M. in munitions factories. Some of them first had to drop off their small children at day-care centers. In towns all across America, six o'clock in the morning would find women, many of them holding crying children, standing on corners waiting for buses. Few people could drive to work any longer. They did not have enough gasoline allowance.

It took time to get all these things under way. Ration boards had to be set up, ration books printed. You stood in line to apply for them. One glass of jelly was a bonus allowed with each book. Any factories had to be readied for war production. I would say it was nearly a year before we felt ourselves "at war."

Was there a black market? Of course. Isn't there always?

There is unfairness during times of both war and peace. It just seems worse during war.

Right after Pearl Harbor many band leaders volunteered for service and went into uniform—Artie Shaw, Eddy Duchin, Orrin Tucker, Claude Thornhill, Rudy Vallee, Glenn Miller, and others. Benny Goodman was turned down because of an old back injury; Kay Kyser, because of his eyes. But Kay set a significant trend when he announced that with the exception of the Lucky Strike radio show, all the band's engagements for the duration would be *donated* to army camps, navy and marine bases, and, most important, hospitals.

So throughout the war we toured extensively, taking movie stars with us whenever we could. There were a few of them who were so loyal that they never refused to drop whatever they were doing and come with us. We could always depend on Bette Davis, Olivia de Havilland, Lucille Ball, and Marlene Dietrich.

We played at the Hollywood Canteen every Saturday night. It was Bette Davis who organized the Canteen, where service men could meet and dance with movie stars. In the beginning she had trouble finding bands available to play Saturdays or willing to play free. But Kay soon pledged our Saturday nights to her.

From 1942 through 1944 the band moved at high speed, playing at camps, bases, hospitals, and the Canteen, and on the Lucky Strike program. We also had a long string of movie-making jobs. In 1942 we made *My Favorite Spy* and in 1943 *Swing Fever, As Thousands Cheer,* and *Around the World.* When Kay went on vacation in 1943, Art Linkletter took over as band leader. In 1944 the band appeared in *Hollywood Canteen* and *Carolina Blues.*

Early in this period, Ginny Simms left the band for a movie career of her own. Georgia Carroll became our girl singer. She was beautiful and talented, a great asset to the band. In 1944 she and Kay were married, and while they were off on a vacation for most of that summer, Phil Harris took over as band leader. Phil was a great person to be around, a natural clown with whom we were all comfortable. Late at night in our bus going home after work, Phil would often put on a performance.

The seats in the old chartered bus we used were worn green leather, and Phil's "audience" sat in the back of the bus, which Phil dubbed the Green Room—an interesting fact, since the room where performers wait today to go on talk shows is called the Green Room. We had our own Green Room years before television came of age, though it was not used for waiting. Each band member had his own corner where the bus would pull up to let him off. When we reached Phil's corner, the whole gang would always say in chorus, "Say hello to Alice, Phil." And he would answer, "Yeah."

Once the war was well into the period when supplies were tight, the color of the American Tobacco Company's package of Lucky Strike cigarettes was changed from green and red to white and red. The green dye used to make the packages was no longer available; it was being used to dye GI uniforms and other army equipment. An order came down from George Washington Hill that our radio commercials were to include the phrase "Lucky Strike green has gone to war."

There was something about this slogan that Kay did not like, and we often talked about it. He felt that it sounded as though American Tobacco Company was taking credit for sending the green dye to war when, actually, the company had no choice in the matter. The dye was simply no longer available for nonmilitary uses. It might seem like a small point, but at that time, it seemed important. The impression created was that giving up the green had been a voluntary sacrifice.

I agreed with Kay, and the next time we were in New York I went with him to see Mr. Hill to complain about the slogan and ask that it be removed from our commercials. When we went into his office, Mr. Hill was sitting behind his desk with his straw hat on. He was a crackerjack of a business man, a shrewd character. His straw hat was a part of him.

He was glad to see us and asked, "What can I do for you boys?" We did our best to cut down the slogan. The gist of our complaint was that it was our program. We had invented it, and though we appreciated Mr. Hill's sponsorship (Kay was most tactful in saying all this), we did not like the expression "Lucky Strike green has gone to war." Might he not consider replacing it with some other slogan?

Mr. Hill said: "Keep talking, boys. Get it all out of your system. Get it said. Say whatever you want." We said it all, in a couple of different ways, and stopped.

"Are you through?" he asked.

"Yes, sir, that's about it. That's what we came to say."

"OK. Now Ish, you come around here on my right side, behind my desk, and stand there. And Kay, you come over here on my left side behind my desk. I want to show you something." We walked around, and he pulled open the left and the right top drawers of his desk simultaneously. At first there seemed to be nothing in either drawer. But there was a piece of cardboard pasted on the wooden bottom of each drawer. Something was printed in big letters.

> LAST YEAR EVERY TIME FIVE PACKAGES OF CIGARETTES WERE SOLD, FOUR OF THEM WERE LUCKY STRIKES.

"Read that, boys," Mr. Hill said. We said we already had.

He shut the drawers and said, "Now you go around to the front of my desk where you were." I felt like we were a couple of little kids. But we went back around, and he looked at us. "Now, what was that you were saying about my advertising methods?"

We just grinned and saluted him. "Well, thanks, Mr. Hill, for seeing us. Thanks for your time." And we turned and walked out, having made not a dent in Mr. Hill. We saw that we were about as influential as the *p* in pneumonia. The slogan stayed in the commercials.

The band, or at least some of us—always with Kay, of course—often had meetings with Mr. Hill to plan the programs or determine policy. Or should I say to agree with him? And in all of Mr. Hill's meetings he loved to dramatize what he said.

One day, high on the thirtieth or fortieth floor of a New York skyscraper, we had a meeting with him. He sat at the end of a long conference table, and the windows were open. He always wore his straw hat, as I have said, not only to these meetings but all day long. It was a hot summer afternoon, and a pleasant breeze was coming through the window to his right. As it turned out, it was a perfect setting for him to make a point.

He asked for suggestions, and when someone came up with one, he took off his fifty-dollar straw hat and sailed it out the window. As we watched, the wind carried it out over the city, and Mr. Hill said, "Gentlemen, just a straw in the wind!" So much for that idea.

At another meeting he asked for opinions from everyone at the table. He kept a big pitcher of drinking water near him, with glasses, and after listening to every man, he stood up and turned the pitcher of water upside down over the conference table. Before the men could gasp, the water was running all over their pants, and Mr. Hill said, "Gentlemen, you're all wet!"

I understand he would repeat these performances in various meetings until they wore thin. Then he would think up something new. This is the same man who, though he loved to put people down, also loved to build them up. He was a many-sided personality, who knew many things.

---

## Shocks and Shells

> As the bomb fell, we saw a whole city disappear. I wrote in my log the words: MY GOD! WHAT HAVE WE DONE?
>
> —Captain Robert Lewis

The band was doing our regular Lucky Strike program at an army camp somewhere in California. The camp theater was brand new, with an exceptionally large stage. Because only men were in the army camps those days, there was a john in the middle of the back brick wall. No walls surrounded it, and it was never seen by the audience, since there were stage draperies in front of it all the time. It was just there, against the wall, big as all outdoors for men backstage to use. I do not recall any complaints about invasion of privacy.

Also backstage during this camp show, which was being broadcast over radio, was an NBC microphone on a stand with a sign:

> ABSOLUTE SILENCE! DO NOT TALK IN THIS AREA AS THIS MICROPHONE WILL BE LIVE DURING THE PROGRAM

In those days I was not necessarily on the stage for the whole hour. There were times when I did not play my horn but had to go on only when I did my jokes with Kay. And Harry had to go on only when he did his vocals. So that night Harry and I were sitting backstage about ten feet from the john and far enough from the mike so that if we whispered to each other when we talked, we knew we would not be heard over the microphone. At station breaks several times during the program the announcer needed to come back to the mike and say, "This is the NBC network" and so forth. The mike had no switch, and that was the reason for keeping it live.

At one point the band was playing, the vocal group was singing a quiet ballad to all the GIs and to millions of people across the country, and Harry and I were sitting back there in a leisurely fashion, taking it all in. Then suddenly we both seemed to have the same thought. We looked at each other and grinned. At a moment when the music was at its softest, we walked to the mike. Harry carefully lifted it off the stand, and we went silently over to the john. I flushed it as Harry lowered the mike just far enough into the bowl to be darned sure the mike would pick up the noise without getting wet.

That was how the sound of a john flushing went out over 440 NBC stations all across the United States that night. Later we heard that the switchboard at NBC in New York lighted up like a Christmas tree. Stations from all over the country called in, saying, "Hey, we hear a john flushing behind the music!"

It was a mystery that caused quite a stir. People talked about it for a long time. No one knew how it could possibly happen. But Harry Babbitt and I knew. It was our secret for years.

In August, 1944, the band went on a nationwide tour on the Sante Fe Train with about thirty top movie stars. The tour was called the Hollywood Band Cavalcade, and its purpose was to raise money through the sale of war bonds. Then in November and December, we did hospital shows—sixty hospitals in sixty days.

There was one hospital where we did an especially good show, we thought. But at the end of the show, when we were used to hearing stupendous applause, there was dead silence. We all lowered our horns and sat stunned. The silence lasted just for a few seconds, but it seemed an eternity. Not until the men began to cheer and holler did we recall that we were in a hospital for double amputees. How the hell are *they* going to applaud? It was a shocker for us. Even though we had known where we were at the beginning of the evening, it was only the silence that brought home to each of us some of the awful consequences of the war. Four or five of the guys in the band suddenly got up and went outside. In a while they were back, pale and fighting tears. Meanwhile I was close to tears myself and felt guilty and embarrassed to be in one piece. I did not know then that I was to feel that way hundreds of times more.

## The Big Step Forward

> Don't look back. Something might be gaining on you.
>
> —Satchel Paige

It was while we were on this hospital tour that I received my "Greetings" from Uncle Sam in some forwarded mail. I was inducted into the army at Fort MacArthur, California, on March 29, 1945. I was just nine months short of being thirty-eight, which would have put me over the age limit for the draft.

The man standing next to me in the induction line, who "stepped forward" at the same time I did, was John Conte, at the time married to movie star Marilyn Maxwell. An officer read to us from a paper, telling us we agreed "that although drafted, you are making this move of your own free will, not coerced, and that you will so indicate by taking one step forward, signifying you do this voluntarily." We would have laughed if it had not been sad. It was reminiscent of the Irishman who said, "I will go to war willingly if compelled to go."

We had been at Fort MacArthur about three weeks when Kay did a show there. I sat in the audience, entertained by a band I was a missing part of, watching the show I had helped do so many times. It was a strange feeling. I was gone, yet here I was. Kay had not yet replaced me, so there was no comedian in the performance. He finally did replace me for a short time, with Jack Douglas, who did his own brand of comedy and wrote his own material.

I was sent to Camp Lee, Virginia, for basic training. A lot of show people went there for fourteen weeks of basic and then moved on to Special Services Training Groups if they were needed. I did not know where I would wind up.

In basic training I quickly learned many things. If you were going to get sick, for example, you had to do it by 7 A.M. or forget it, because you were allowed to sign the sick book only at 7 A.M. If you became sick during the day and had not signed the sick book, then you were not sick. I also learned:

> If it lays there, pick it up.
> If you can't pick it up, paint it white.
> If it moves, salute it.

We slept alphabetically. When I arrived at the Camp Lee barracks, I discovered that the man a cot or two away from mine was the famous boxer Buddy Baer, Max's brother. Both of us were *B*'s—Baer and Bogue—up on the second floor. There were fifty men in each building. I was glad to see Buddy in my group. I had never met him before, but we hit it off at once. We hung around together all during basic.

We were supposed to eat only in our assigned mess halls. But Buddy got sick of the food, and one day he said we should go to another one. So we went to a mess hall half a mile away and walked in. The guys recognized us, especially Buddy, and welcomed us. Even the cook looked pleased. It was a big deal for them to have Buddy Baer there. There were forty-eight different mess halls at Camp Lee, and during our stint there, I don't think we missed many of them.

Buddy's idea always was: "If you want something, try it. You'll usually get away with it, because people will go along with you. Act like you're perfectly within your rights, and everyone will figure you know what you're doing." Sometimes we walked into a mess hall forty-five minutes before it was to open, and as if ordering in a restaurant, Buddy would tell the cook to fix our eggs "over, not too well done," and ask for lots of coffee. The guy would give us a funny look, but he would do as Buddy said. Buddy was incredibly persuasive.

He had a sleeping problem. The cots were six feet long and not too comfortable at that. Several inches of Buddy dangled over the edge and there was no way he could sleep. He tried it for a week or so and then complained to his commanding officer: "I've got to have a longer cot."

"There aren't any longer ones. You'll just have to make do," he was told.

"The hell with that. I've got to have a longer bed. I've got to have some sleep!"

"I already told you . . ."

"Tell you what you do," said Buddy, unperturbed. "Give me a weekend pass every weekend, and I'll go to Richmond and pay my own way. I'll find a hotel with a long bed or else get a double bed so I can sleep at an angle. And on Friday, Saturday, and Sunday nights I'll get some sleep and can suffer here the rest of the week."

When the army said OK to that, I was flabbergasted. But Buddy was not finished. "But I can't go by myself," he said. "I've got to have somebody with me. Let me take Ish Kabibble along." The army finally agreed he should have company. So Baer and I went to Richmond on weekends and had all kinds of fun. Monday morning would arrive, and we were supposed to be back at Camp Lee. A few times Buddy said: "The hell with it. Let's take a couple of extra days."

Of course, that made us AWOL. Buddy would say, "Well, they aren't out looking for us yet." And it was probably true. They knew what hotel we stayed in, and they generally did not do anything for a few days. On Wednesday or Thursday we would walk in just like nothing had happened. The officers were always giving us a bad time anyway, as they did all show people. They called us Hollywood jerks.

So Buddy would walk in, with me right behind him, and before the sergeant could say, "Where the hell have you Hollywood jerks been? You're AWOL!" Buddy would say: "Have we had any phone calls? Has Bob Hope been calling me again? Has President Roosevelt been trying to reach me? Well, if any of those people call, we'll be over in the barracks. The trip down from Richmond was exhausting. Ish and I are going to get a little shut-eye, but if any of those guys—like Bing Crosby or Paul Whiteman—calls us, you'll know where to find us."

So at six feet seven inches, Buddy got away with a lot of stuff that the ordinary guy could not get away with. He always had a flip answer. Once a sergeant got so mad at Buddy's attitude that he flung Buddy's passes at him and yelled: "Here! Get out of here and never come back!" When we did not return till Thursday that week, the sergeant began, "What do you guys mean by . . ." Buddy opened his eyes wide and answered, "But Sergeant, you ordered us *never* to come back!" The sergeant was tongue-tied.

The camp hospital would ask anybody who had a name at all to go talk with the boys in the wards. These fellows were not wounded, just sick temporarily, perhaps with flu, or maybe they had broken a bone in training, something like that. Buddy and I went to the hospital wards together, and we walked through the ward, introducing ourselves and talking with the men about anything they wanted to talk about.

Then Buddy suggested: "Why don't we work up a little act? You be the comedian, and I'll be the straight man. We could do a fighter routine, maybe. I know a lot of fighter jokes. It'll be better than just walking through the wards."

Not long before this, Buddy had fought Joe Louis, then the world's champion, in Madison Square Garden, and Louis had knocked him out in the fourth round. Joe Louis was not nearly so tall as Buddy. So as part of our act I asked him, "When you got in the ring, where did Joe come to on you?" Buddy pointed to his chin. "Right about there and too damned often, too. Man could that guy hit! After a few wallops, I tell you, I wanted to jump out of that ring and run headlong for Times Square. He scared the living daylights out of me, and by the fourth round, I knew there was no way I was going to lick him."

The act that we worked out was not too bad. At the beginning I would walk onstage with the bangs down—the dumb guy—and say: "Good evenings, fellas. I'm glad to be here tonight. As you all know, I'm a famous boxer, and I've whipped an awful lot of boxers." And I pulled out a list of names on adding-machine paper that would unfurl clear to the floor. "I'll read you the names of a few of the famous boxers I've whipped during my day," I went on. The sick guys would laugh because I was so skinny and obviously not a fighter. I read my list: "Luis Firpo, John L. Sullivan, Jack Dempsey, Joe Louis, Jess Willard, Max Baer and his brother Buddy . . ." Meanwhile, supposedly unknown to me, Buddy had walked onstage and was standing behind me. The audience was clapping, applauding Buddy, but naturally I thought that they were applauding my fighting record, and I bowed my acknowledgment and then went on: "Let's see, where was I? Oh yes, Buddy Baer, Max Schmelling . . ."

At this point Buddy tapped me on the shoulder and came around beside me to ask, "What is that you're reading there?"

"This? Oh, this is a list of fighters I've whipped." I am six feet tall, so Buddy stood seven inches above me. He looked down at me and said, "Read that again, those last two names at the end."

"Oh, Buddy Baer, Max Schmelling . . ." He stopped me and turned me around so that I was facing him. With one hand he grasped me by my shirt under my chin and lifted me seven inches off the floor, which brought my nose right up to his nose, and he said: "My name is Buddy Baer, and you've never licked me, and you never *will* lick me. You *can't* lick me." Then he pushed me away from him and set me gently down onto the floor. I turned to the audience, pulled a pencil from behind my ear, and said, "OK, so I'll erase that one."

The routine went on. Next I might say: "I'm still a fighter. I've got two strong socks, one on each foot. And I'll never forget when I fought the champion, a short fellow with a bald head. It was the third round before I realized he wasn't in the ring yet and I'd been fighting the stool."

So Buddy and I did our fighter routine around Camp Lee in the hospitals until finally it was decided that we were to go to other camps to do our show. We never knew where we were going till we got there. One day we found ourselves at Camp Pickett. We were glad because we had heard that Red Skelton was in one of the hospitals there and we were anxious to see him. We both knew him from Hollywood days. But we could not find Red. Finally we had entertained every ward, and still there was no Red. So we asked about him and learned that, at his own request, he was in a special ward, under lock and key, with thirteen mental patients.

Red had been in the Army for some time, entertaining on troop ships shuttling back and forth from Europe. Only about two hundred men could crowd into the ship's auditorium at one time, so he had done fifteen to eighteen shows a day, a pace that no one could keep up for long. One day, as he got off a ship in New York, he collapsed on the pier from sheer exhaustion. Taken to Camp Pickett for a complete rest, he was hounded by autograph seekers, signing his name for some guys over and over, sometimes twenty-five or thirty times. So he asked to be put someplace where no one could get at him, and when he heard of this special ward of thirteen men, he asked to be moved there.

There was an office at either end of the ward, and the hospital gave one of them to Red. He slept in it. He also painted pictures like only he can paint, and he became acquainted with the other men in the ward.

When the hospital aide unlocked the door to let us into the ward, Red saw us and ran toward us, glad to see us but wondering why we were there. We told him we had come to do our show for him and the other fellows.

Red took us into the ward, introduced us, and then flopped on the nearest bed and said: "OK, you guys. It's great to see you again. Go ahead and entertain us."

Red knows every joke in the book. If you start a joke, he can finish it. That was what he did that day. For almost every joke we set up, he said the punch line before Buddy and I could get to it.

Finally Red said, "Now you guys get in bed, and I'll entertain *you.*" So we changed places. Red had rehearsed a "straight" named Smitty from among the patients, and the two of them quickly had us all in stitches, and I don't mean hospital stitches.

We looked at Red's paintings. He had a pair he had finished and framed that I fell hard for. One of them was a portrait of an Englishman with a Van Dyke beard. Red had not drawn the man's body or even his neck, and underneath the beard was a man's white hospital urinal, commonly called a duck. Red had a brass plate on the frame reading, "MAN WITH DUCK." The other picture was identical to the first except that underneath the beard there was nothing. Thus, the name of this one was "MAN WITHOUT DUCK."

How I wanted those pictures. This was, of course, long before Red's paintings became famous and expensive. I said to him: "I do paintings, too, Red. I've got a pair at home that I did of two pool tables '8-ball in the Corner Pocket' and '8-Ball in the Side Pocket.' Gee, I wish we could trade or something." He replied: "OK, why not? After the war, when we get back to Hollywood, call me up and we'll trade."

The first time I saw him after the war was one night at a benefit we were doing at the Ambassador Hotel. We relived some of those "basic days," and that was when I asked about the paintings. But he said his wife Georgia had fallen in love with them and would not part with them. I did not blame her at all. They were true works of art.

I have no desire to relive the bad features of basic training. Basic is something that has to be done; a soldier has to be trained. Anyone who has been through it knows what it is like. Anyone who has not probably wouldn't believe it all: the blistered feet, the snakes, the thirsts denied water, the endurance tests, and so forth. But there were good memories to take home, and sometimes too, we even had fun.

One of the first things we learned in basic was to empty our barracks fast. But no matter how fast we would dash out of that building every morning and get in line, it was never fast enough to suit the sergeant.

According to the routine, we were to sit on our cots with our helmets on, and when the sergeant blew his whistle, we were to tear out of the building on the double and be lined up before he blew his whistle the second time. Of course, we never got there on time, because he blew his second whistle while we were still coming out the door. He would complain vehemently and at some length. Then he told us to go back in, sit back on our cots, and this time leave the helmets and strap our water canteens to our belts. "And gentlemen," he said, "when I blow the whistle this time, don't you even bother to open that front door. Just bring the screen door right with you."

About the third day we got sick of this treatment, and late that night we loosened the screws on the screen door. Next morning when he gave his impossible orders, we came tearing out of the building with the screen door and laid it at the sergeant's feet. As we lined up, not one of us even cracked a smile.

Nearly every barracks had its own little dog. A stray dog showed up looking for food, stayed, and in time attached itself to a group of men in a certain building. One of these dogs slept under our steps. He had a stick about three feet long that he kept under the steps with him. When we lined up, he stood at the head of the line beside us. If we had our rifles, he had his stick in his mouth. If we took the rifles back to the barracks, he took his stick and laid it under the steps. At roll call, when we barked out "Here!" he laid his stick down, barked once, in his turn, and picked up the stick again. He marched with us and did everything else with us. He was one of us.

---

## A-1 Priority

First it rained
And then it snew
And then it friz
And then it thew
And then it snew again.
—Ish

Although after basic I was transferred to a Special Services Training Group (89th Company) at Camp Lee, I was never to get that training. After the training, I was to be sent to Europe. But it was June, 1945, and the war was over in Europe. So I asked to be sent to the Pacific.

"Are you crazy?" I was asked. "There's a war going on over there!"

"But I don't want to go where it's all over. Isn't the Pacific where the GIs will want entertainment?"

While they were deciding what to do with me, a week or so passed, and then I heard something was afoot. I did not know what. But one day a jeep drove alongside me. The driver asked, "Private Bogue?" "Yes, sir," I replied. "Get in!" he said. Without any explanation I was flown to New York, where I reported to a Major Richards with Special Services at 47 West 47th Street. He told me that General Douglas MacArthur had issued orders that I be flown to Manila immediately. But that sounded so preposterous that I could not believe it until I had heard the whole story.

Kay Kyser had gone to the Pacific with three girls from MGM, assembled a small band from a navy band stationed in Manila, and had rehearsed a show for the GIs. The first time they performed was for General MacArthur at Clark Field in Manila. After the show, General MacArthur talked to Kay and asked: "Where's Ish Kabibble? I saw you in New York, and he was with you. He should be over here. Where is he?"

"I don't know where he is now, General," said Kay. "You have him in your army somewhere in the States." The upshot of it was that MacArthur issued orders that I be found and delivered to Manila to join Kay for the duration of his tour.

My orders read that I was to have an A-1 priority seat. So it was. New York to Hamilton Field, California, a tearful goodbye to Janet, then on to Honolulu, Guam, and Manila. Once we were on the plane and airborne, the steward said: "We will eat our lunch at halfway mark to Hawaii. We will smoke three men at a time, up forward, grouped around a cup of water."

On June 29, 1945, at 7 P.M. we landed at Nichols Field in Manila. I was met by a sergeant named Hank, in a jeep. He drove me through certain sections of the city to show me some of the damage wrought by the war. It is impossible to describe. No building had escaped shelling by Japanese ships or bombing by their planes. Walls sloped at all angles, and beautiful concrete buildings were gutted by fire and repeated bombings. Manila was dusty and hot, and army vehicles tied traffic in knots. The only building that had been partially repaired was City Hall, part of which housed MacArthur's headquarters. Altogether we drove through about ten miles of bombed and burned city. We passed an eight-block-long line of GIs waiting to get in what was left of a movie house showing *Back to Bataan.*

Hank took me to what he called an officers' club. It had once been a wealthy Filipino's home. Now it was gutted, and only parts of any room were usable. All the glass in the windows was gone; four-inch lizards ran over the walls and ceilings catching bugs and little squeaking insects. The bed I was to use had netting on it. That was where I slept for one night. Kay had stayed in this room, I was told. He had then gone to Zamboanga, where the monkeys have no tails.

I was to be flown to Zamboanga the next day to meet Kay. It was a two-and-a-half-hour plane ride south, six hundred miles or more, they told me.

At six the next morning a sergeant shook me awake. "Captain Simon is on the phone," he said. The captain told me he would pick me up in twenty minutes. I waited three hours. Another case of "Hurry up and wait." At ten o'clock a Lieutenant Watson picked me up in a jeep, explaining: "We have to fly down this morning. This is monsoon weather, and storms start up around four in the afternoon."

At eleven we took off from Birdson-Neilson Airfield in a B-25 that belonged to General W. D. Styer. When I climbed into the plane, I was surprised to find there was only one seat behind the pilot's, and the whole bottom of the plane was glass or what appeared to be glass. I knew about glass bottoms in boats, but not in planes. The seat was like a barber's chair. General Styer commanded the parachute troops. He sat in the barber chair and flew way above the planes that dropped the paratroops, directing their operations from high in the air, with binoculars, looking down through the glass floor.

So I, Mern Bogue, of Erie, Pennsylvania, rode in that barber chair all the way down to Zamboanga, seeing everything below me without craning my neck. When we got there, we had to land on the beach, since the runway had been bombed. When we hit the beach, a jeep rushed up, and the driver said, "Private Bogue?" and I, of course, said, "Yes, sir!" He said "Get in," and I got in.

We taxied down the beach toward a huddled group of about twenty persons about half a mile away. I soon saw that some of them were black people with their faces painted chalk white. They carried big spears and wore fancy headdresses. Later I learned they were Maori natives. They were gathered around a small group that included Kay.

The jeep pulled up right in front of Kay, and sensing the drama of the occasion, I stood up, put my hand in my coat like Napoleon, and said, "Dr. Livingstone, I presume?" Kay bowed to the Sad Sack who had arrived in the general's B-25, the Man with the Bangs and the A-1 priority. So went the Kyser-Kabibble reunion!

## GIs and Generals

It is easy to be brave from a safe distance.

—Aesop

Kay and his troupe had landed on the beach at Zamboanga only a short time before our B-25 did. We drove to General J. A. Doe's quarters; he was commanding officer of the 41st Division. We had rooms in his house, which was the only unbombed building in Zamboanga. It even had a john that flushed—the first one I had seen in the Philippines. Naturally Kay had put together a good show. The girls were nice kids, very clean-cut, and the GI audiences, I learned, thought they were great.

We did some shows in the area before we left Zamboanga. One was a hospital show that opened my eyes to how bad hospital conditions can be. The windows were bombed out. Birds, insects, and bats flew around the rooms with no regard for the rows of wounded GIs who lay in the cots below, unable to duck. The patients had a stare that I will never forget. It seemed to say: "What a hole to wind up in—and I started out from Brooklyn to win this war myself."

I could hardly look at them. Who was I that I should be able to walk and get out of there after the show? And there were the nurses. How could they get nurses to work in such filth and heat and under such conditions? They kept at their work all during the show, at times almost running. They looked like typical American girls, but they had a fixed expression, as though they were steeling themselves to keep going. Maybe it was a tired expression. I wondered how long they had been there.

When we left, I felt small and guilty. Compared with what those nurses were doing and what those GIs were going through, my efforts to make them laugh a little for a few minutes of one day of their lives seemed no contribution at all.

We did two shows a day throughout the Philippines. At Cebu, one of the men came backstage to introduce himself. He had just finished a show for one of the divisions that had helped take Okinawa about two months before. "My name is Lloyd

Muth," said the GI, "and I'm from Erie, and I know your sister Christine." My face must have shown I was pleased as punch, and we had a good talk. He gave me a Japanese flag he had gotten on Okinawa.

Rain never fazed the men. Once during a downpour I was on the stage, and I looked down on the first eight or ten rows of men, where there was a low spot. Under raincoats and ponchos the guys were sitting on benches covered with muddy water, which meant that they were in water up to their equators. But they were laughing away all the same. Not a one of them seemed aware of the water they were sitting in.

Occasionally there was a part of a day when no show was scheduled. Then I would often go down on the beach or into the bulrushes where there might be half a dozen men on some kind of guard duty, and I would visit with them for an hour or so. Afterward I would have names in my pocket and a lump in my throat. The names were of families I was to telephone when I got home.

Because I was with Kay, I met, dined with, and got to know several generals during our tour. General Walter Krueger I will always think of warmly, because he was so kind to me. He had his headquarters at San Fernando, where we met him. He commanded the 6th Army, and many say he is the man who really won the Pacific war. He received us in his office, which was an old Filipino home that General Arthur MacArthur had lived in when he was stationed in the Philippines at the turn of the century.

General Krueger talked so softly that it was difficult to hear him. When we met him, he was sixty-five, but a tough guy. We visited with him that day for half an hour, and then he asked us to stay for dinner. Practically all the brass in the islands was to be there also. I said to him during a lull that I thought I should leave, since I would be the only private in the group. But he insisted I stay, adding: "Don't feel out of place. Tonight you are a welcome guest in my house." But I did feel somewhat out of place. I waited at the table until all fifteen generals were seated, and then I took a seat as far away from General Krueger as possible. He kept smiling at me all through dinner. He left the table after we ate, and returned and gave me a picture of himself inscribed, "To Merwin Bogue from Walter Krueger, General, U.S. Army."

General R. L. Eichelberger commanded the 8th Army, and we probably saw him more than we did any of the other generals. He was a good friend. Kay told him that when the war was over, we were going to give a big party for him in Hollywood and invite any stars he wished to be there. After the war, we had the party at the Beverly Hills Club. The two people he especially wanted to meet and talk with, he said, were Billie Dove and William S. Hart. Billie Dove came, but unfortunately Hart was too ill to attend. General Eichelberger spent most of the evening talking with Billie Dove and also with Janet. The next day the papers reported, "General Eichelberger spent most of the evening talking with young starlets." This amused Janet, and you can bet your life it amused Billie Dove.

After a show on Leyte, we went for a ride on General Eichelberger's rescue boat, passing the battleships *Mississippi*, *Arkansas*, and *Texas*. When we pulled near the *Mississippi*, members of the crew leaned over the rail, and we moved close and talked back and forth. I combed my hair down in bangs, and some guys yelled: "Hey Ish! How's the Blackhawk in Chicago?" and "Hiya, Ish! How's the Paramount in L.A.?" It was the same when we pulled over next to the *Arkansas*. But when we pulled close to the *Texas*, there was not a glance our way. The men were all lined up for inspection. We circled the ship three times, but the crew were not allowed to turn a head. Imagine how long it had been since they had set eyes on three American girls and how bad they must have wanted to steal a quick look. But not a head turned. Finally Kay grabbed a microphone and yelled, "Oh, come on, Admiral, have a heart!" But nothing happened, so we went on to the next ship, which was named the *Relief*.

The number of men fighting the war continually astounded me. Driving from one show to the next, the dust in the roads from troop movements was so thick that it choked us. We rode in jeeps with handkerchiefs or some other cloth over our faces, looking like bandits.

We flew to Batangas in southern Luzon. Jeeps from General Joseph Swing's 11th Airborne Division picked us up. We had lunch with him, with chocolate sundaes for dessert, way out here in the jungle, which made us feel guilty again.

We drove sixty-five miles on bad roads through the jungle to the 1st Cavalry Division and did a show from 5 to 6:30 P.M. The boys had been waiting since 2 P.M., and that alone, without thinking about the war they had to fight, was enough to make us cringe. Every time broken-down jeeps or bad planning made us hours late for a show, we found it embarrassing.

Next a plane took us to Lingayen, and then we had a four-hour jeep ride to Baguio, thirty miles from the front, where we did a show for the men who were doing the actual fighting. The ride to Baguio was unbelievable. The first fifty miles was flat country. On both sides the road was littered with cars, trucks, and tanks, all blown up and shoved into the rice paddies. At crossroads a dozen or so tanks would be left where the two sides had fought it out. Some of the tanks were ours; others were Japanese. The tanks kept reminding us that there are two sides to a war.

After the first fifty miles, we hit a steep mountain trail, on which we passed hundreds of caves that were, I later learned, similar to ones on Okinawa. They had been dug by the Filipinos and were later occupied by the Japanese. Each cave had five or six entrances. We, the Americans, had blasted the entrances shut, with Japanese inside. Later we went back, opening up the caves to find papers we needed. It was all "we" and "they." I was learning about war.

The road to Baguio was so steep and so rough that the jeeps barely made it. No one familiar with the territory seemed surprised.

Baguio was famed as the vacation spot of the Philippines. That seemed ironic, since it was now leveled from bombing, completely ruined except for the country club and a couple of mansions. At the country club we met General Eichelberger, General Oscar Griswold (who was from Erie), and several other generals. The club was the command post closest to the fighting. It also served as a rest camp for men with skin diseases brought on by the heat. One of them was a Sigma Chi from my West Virginia days, a guy named Brownie who was a major.

We did a 7:30 show and then went to the officers' club, where we heard a second report about the atomic bomb. We had first heard of it on August 8, when we were with the 11th Airborne. Now, on Monday, August 13, we heard a report from San Francisco. I was standing near General Griswold when the radio announced, "General Griswold's flyers at Baguio today dropped leaflets on General Yamashito's quarters telling him to give up." General Griswold sort of nodded, as if he agreed. So I knew the report was true. To that point we had heard nothing official. General Yamashito and his two thousand men were surrounded in a valley about thirty miles north of us.

General Eichelberger took Kay and me to see his 8th Army headquarters, which was located in a mansion of thirty or forty rooms up on a hill. Its verandas overlooked the valleys where the fighting was going on. The mahogany and cherry teakwood walls were magnificent, though bullet holes were all over the house dating from the time our flyers strafed it to get Yamashito out. We sat in General Eichelberger's bedroom, where he had an icebox rigged up from which we ate cold fresh pineapple slices.

After that we went back to the country club and to bed. We each had a canvas cot, a GI can of water, and a helmet to wash in. The Japanese had destroyed all furniture and plumbing, doing everything they could to make it hard for Americans to use the house.

Up at seven the next morning, we took off in jeeps again, back down the same highway that we had come up with such difficulty. It was easy to go down. But we knew that it had taken our forces 120 days to fight their way up that winding trail to Baguio.

That night, during a short intermission in our show, someone came running up to Kay backstage with a message that read, "Japan ready to accept Potsdam ultimatum." After some discussion among the top officers present, it was decided to withhold the news from the men until after the show. It was Kay who read them the message. I never heard such yelling. The men hugged one another and jumped up and down. The band played like it had never played before, and for about twenty minutes we watched those guys be happy beyond measure, which was a great sight. Afterward General Maxwell

Murray invited us to his quarters, where he broke open a bottle of Australian scotch that he had saved for celebrating the war's end. We did away with it in short order.

The tour continued. The Allies still had not accepted the Japanese surrender. The girls were all sick. One was in the hospital with a fractured backbone. Some overactive jitterbug partner had twisted her back. Another of the girls had hay fever, and the third one had a cold and an infected throat. I was OK. Iron Man Kabibble they were calling me. But I had to keep powdering up to stop the jungle rot that was trying to get me. My skin was peeling just from constantly being wet with perspiration. I was never dry; even when I slept, I was wringing wet.

News bulletins reported wild celebrations in the States; they also reported that the consensus of opinion there was to continue the war. The boys around me said: "Let *them* come over and finish it then. We want to go home."

At Bagabag, not far from where Yamashito was cornered, we did a show on a stage that had just been built that same day. Ten thousand men sat on the ground in a sort of natural amphitheater. Two thousand of them had come in that day from the front lines to see the show.

There was one man in particular whom I will never forget. He was from Rocky Mount, North Carolina, Kay's hometown, and he came backstage to see Kay. He was so tired he could hardly stay awake. He talked with his eyes shut. He was caked with mud clear up to his neck. He had been in the front lines for thirty-one consecutive days and had to go back the next day. I commented that the war was about over, but he did not even look up. He just said, "Oh," and then, after a minute, he added: "It may be so, but all I know is I'm still liable to get killed—like the two who got it yesterday. Those two empty cots don't look to me like the war's over." He figured Yamashito would keep on fighting.

I could not think of a single encouraging word for him. I couldn't even say "I know" or "I understand," because I didn't know and I didn't understand. Even though I was surrounded by talk of the war and by its victims, I was not *living* it.

The roads in the Philippines generally ran the long way of the islands and close to the beaches. Rice paddies were everywhere.

The army had been forced to find dry ground for camps, which meant that some units were scattered over an area of twenty or thirty square miles.

Army traffic had pulverized the dirt roads into powder. It got in your hair and eyes, and sweat ran down your face and body in black streams. Dust had covered many Filipino houses until they were not fit to live in. Hundreds of little children lined the roads and held up two fingers in the shape of a V, and when we rode by, they smiled and said, "Victory, Joe." To them, all GIs were "Joe." They went to school and got dressed up all fancy when they did. It was a surprise to see them in spotless white, going to school through the dust and the filthy puddles.

One day I took a shower in a field by a stream and saw a 250-power unexploded aerial bomb lying there, right where it fell. Was it a dud? I asked a GI if it was still dangerous. "Not so long as it doesn't go off," he said.

"Why hasn't it been hauled away and destroyed?"

"We're too busy fighting up ahead. We'll get to it later." I dried myself a little faster and got out of there.

I thought of a line in the Ish Kabibble song: "Get used to it, get used to it." The officers and men I talked with seemed to take all the danger in stride, but I found it hard to get used to.

I kept meeting Texans. There were a lot of them in the army, but then, there's a lot of Texas. General Murray was from Texas. One day he quipped: "Never ask a man where he's from. If he's from Texas, he'll tell you, and if he isn't, then why embarrass him?"

On August 14, 1945, we left northern Luzon and flew to Manila, arriving at the officers' club at 9:30 P.M. At 10 P.M. President Truman was supposed to broadcast some news from Washington. We listened, but no news reached us. So we went to bed.

The next morning we woke up to the sound of people outside yelling, "The war's over!" Kay and I sat up in our cots and looked at each other. In a tired voice Kay said, "Ish, the war's over." I said, "Good," and we both flopped back in bed. We had been expecting it, and of course we were glad, but we were heavy in the gut for all we had seen over there. I lay on my cot thinking about the guys who, like the scared boy from Rocky Mount, were probably still fighting, war over or not, about the fellows in hospitals who would never go home whole, and about those beyond even that. I closed my eyes and saw all the faces in all the audiences of all our shows. Every face had a family wanting him home; every man had a place he cried to be. Kay had to be feeling the same thing I was.

Some GIs got drunk and looked happy. Some looked sullen and said: "What do you mean 'over'? I'm not home, am I?"

As planned, we did our August 16 show at Rizal Stadium. At first the lights kept going out. A private climbed to the top of a pole and held the wires together for three hours, getting terrible burns. He was awarded a Gold Star.

But the war was over. Was it not?

---

## The Ways of War

> One should never do anything that one cannot talk about after dinner.
>
> —Oscar Wilde

Soon after V-J Day we had a day off, and Major Gerald Graham, General MacArthur's aide and a North Carolina boy Kay knew, took us shopping. I got some things to take home—shoes for Janet and my little girls and a Japanese flag for Pete.

At 7:30 that night we had dinner at General Eichelberger's quarters—which were in a beautiful house that was not bombed, because it was owned by a Japanese collaborator. General Eichelberger had just been appointed commander of the entire occupation move into Japan. He was to dictate the where and how of it. We begged him to let us go with him to Tokyo to do some shows, but he insisted that there could be unforeseen problems in Tokyo for some time.

We left Manila for northern Luzon to do a show for the 33rd Division, which was still fighting because the Japanese would not give up. Once hatred is turned on, you can't just turn it off like you would a spigot. Even so, when we arrived, we found some enlisted men having a big victory party under some palm trees. But they were still going to have to fight.

That night I slept alone in a tent in a coconut grove. There was no room for me in the building where the others were. So I was told to sleep on the high tier of bunks—the third tier—to keep clear of Japanese knives, which at night sometimes went "chop chop" into bunks that could be reached from the outside. I did not sleep much, thinking about that. We were so close to the fighting. I dreamed they had slipped into my tent. I lay awake most of the night hearing things. At last I dressed, got my bayonet, and just sat on my bed until 5 A.M. We all had to get up at five anyway, to go back to Manila.

It was still dark. No flashlights were allowed, and I would not have turned one on for anything. At five o'clock I knew it was time for me to start through the palm groves to the mess hall about half a mile away. And I was alone. Scared? I ran from tree to tree, huddling a few seconds against each tree, listening. I bet I listened so hard that morning that my ears were three feet long. Finally, I made one last dash to the mess hall door, then slowed down and entered, trying to appear nonchalant and under control, which I certainly was not.

We rode thirty-five miles in jeeps and got a plane for Manila. On arrival we went directly to General George Kennan's house at Fort McKinley. He had been an ace flyer in World War I and was now commander of the entire Far Eastern Air Force. We asked him about going home and also about going to Tokyo to entertain the GIs who would soon be there. Kay could not give up the Tokyo idea. But General Kennan said that all planes were tied up for the move into Japan—even the Air Transport Command planes. We could not go home, he said, until he released ATC planes, which he would do on September 1. And we could not go to Tokyo—not now or in the near future.

So Kay requested two C-47s to take us to Okinawa to do sixteen extra shows there. The general said that he surely needed and wanted the shows. Later that day, he gave us his permission.

We left for the dock to get a boat to Corregidor. The whole troupe was going, including the girls. We were to go through the famous tunnel where General Jonathan Wainwright had surrendered to the Japanese—the tunnel our soldiers had sealed off with Japanese inside and reopened later. By coincidence our trip to Corregidor was the same day the radio announced that General Wainwright had been found in China.

In the harbor on the way we saw a white Red Cross ship—a

Japanese one that had obviously been captured by the Americans. We got permission to go aboard. The young captain told us the story. A week before, near Wake Island, they had seen several Japanese Red Cross ships, and for some reason this one looked suspicious. Two destroyers were ordered to investigate. On board, the Americans found ammunition and fake patients. The ship was seized and taken to Moratai, where the Japanese were unloaded.

Now the ship was lying off Manila, and we were on it. We were shown through and told to help ourselves to souvenirs. I took a Japanese officer's shoulder bag, a Red Cross shoulder bag, several Japanese books, some Japanese cigarettes, and a canvas kit containing a full set of tools for dismantling Japanese machine guns. I smoked one of the cigarettes. Very mild, it tasted like burnt straw.

Then we went below to the mess hall, holding our noses because of the stench, and into a room full of machine guns, rifles, and grenades. There were great stores of ammunition in boxes marked "MEDICAL SUPPLIES." Everything of any value was marked with that label. A few days later, when I went to the MacArthur home with Major Graham on an errand, Mrs. MacArthur told me that she had recovered her complete silver service a week before from a Manila warehouse. It had been in a crate marked "MEDICAL SUPPLIES" and was addressed ready for shipping to General Yamashito, in case the Japanese won the war. Other boxes, she said, were shipped to her marked the same, but when opened, they were found to be filled with Japanese money meant for General Yamashito.

After disembarking from the Red Cross ship, we went on to Corregidor in a driving rainstorm. Then we were loaded into an open truck. We had no raincoats and so were drenched to our skins.

The entrance to the tunnel was an opening just large enough to allow one person at a time to slide down the dirt into the darkness. The GI in charge explained how we should go through—lined up in single file so as not to get lost in the dark. There were nine of us. The leader had a flashlight, and I took the rear position with another flashlight. Those were the only flashlights we had. Kay was second in line.

The guide asked him: "Do you want to go in some of the

inner passageways?" Kay said: "Certainly! That's what we came for!" Then the guide told us that there might be some Japanese still living way back in there. "But they won't bother us and we won't bother them," he continued, "unless they start throwing grenades." That made me think "Holy mackerel!"

I was the last to slide down the dirt. Once I was in, the odor of the dead bodies almost floored me. One of the girls turned sick and said, "Let me out of here!" and scrambled back above ground. We stayed near the entrance for several minutes to get accustomed to the smell and the whole situation. As we stood there, I played the flashlight around and counted thirty-five or more decayed bodies—mostly bones and maggots—right near us. I wondered, "What are we doing here?"

Soon we moved on. We tried not to step on bodies but could not always avoid it. I pointed the flashlight toward the middle of the group most of the time, so that they could see, since they did not have any light.

Squash. I stepped on something slippery. The awful smell hit me, and I looked down to discover that I had stepped into a man's chest. Now I *knew* I should have stayed out, but it was too late. I was already in, and it was too dark to turn back.

In a side tunnel we heard footsteps. Our whole line stood rigid, listening. Someone was coming toward us. Our guide called out, "Who's there?" Then came a scream. After a moment, a shaky voice said: "It's us—two sailors, looking for souvenirs." What a relief! We had scared the living daylights out of them, since they thought they were alone in the tunnel. From that point on, we all stayed together, as their flashlight had given out.

The tunnel was a mass of bodies, ammunition ("Some yet unexploded," observed our guide), and odd pieces of machinery lying around. You did not know where to step.

Back out in the open air we took deep breaths and said nothing. We picked up our sick girl and got into the truck to go back to our boat. It was still raining. The smell clung to our drenched uniforms. None of us discussed what we had seen. We were too stunned and too sick. It was an education in the ways of war.

On the way back to our quarters, we stopped for mail, and at last I had three letters from Janet! It was the first mail I had received since my arrival in the Philippines. I read them in the pouring rain. She had written others, but the mail would pile up in remote places and be delayed or lost. During the war mail was truly wonderful stuff, more to be wished for than a fine meal or a bunch of money.

## The Corncob Pipe

> There is no security on this earth. There is only opportunity.
>
> —General Douglas MacArthur

Peace was almost at hand. We heard that the signers of peace were gathering. Then a surprise order came from General MacArthur directing Kay and me to be at Manila's City Hall the next morning at eight sharp.

He had not said why he wanted to see us. I had thought it a routine visit; possibly he was just going to tell us goodbye. But when I arrived, I soon saw that we were not the only ones who had been sent for. The lobby outside the general's office was filled with high-ranking brass—generals and admirals from Europe and from all over the Pacific. They were all there in full dress, in their best bibs and tuckers and with their stars, ribbons, and other decorations. Among those present were Lord Mountbatten, General Eichelberger, General Krueger, General Stilwell, and Admiral Halsey. They were apparently all waiting to see MacArthur. I wondered if we had to wait until the general had seen all these important people, since it would be hard for us to do that and get to our navy base show at Cavite, across Manila Bay, by the 2 P.M. show time.

Then I suddenly panicked. I realized I was "out of dress"—no tie, no jacket, with not exactly a dressy set of fatigues. My shoes were not polished up to snuff. I could be thrown in jail. But we had not been told of the importance of this occasion. And it had been common practice for officers, even generals, to walk around Manila without their stars or decorations. They wore fatigues, as they did during battles. There was always the chance that the Japanese were watching from a distance through binoculars, and they would pick off the brass first if the brass could be identified.

Smack on the arrival of eight o'clock, Major Graham, General MacArthur's aide, came out of the general's office, looked around the room, and announced in a loud voice: "Kay Kyser and Private Bogue, the supreme commander will see you now." I do not know whether anyone looked at us in surprise. I kept my eyes straight ahead as Kay and I walked into the general's office, embarrassed to be going ahead of such important men.

The Manila City Hall had been partially bombed out, and General MacArthur's office and lobby were repaired but not what one would call elegantly furnished. The office was a large room containing only one desk and three or four chairs.

Out in the lobby I had felt like the country-bumpkin "slick-sleeve" private that I looked, but General MacArthur made me feel comfortable. He shook hands with us and told us to sit down. "Let's visit," he said, as he lighted up his famous corn-cob pipe. He told us that he had not had a day's vacation in a long time but now was allowed the luxury of taking his thoughts off the war with Japan. So he had scheduled that day to say thank you.

"Now don't you be concerned about my time," he said. "The men out there don't mind waiting. They're here to be thanked, to get a pat on the back, to get brownie points. They'll wait." He thanked Kay for coming over to do the Philippine tour and for doing the extra shows we were not required to do. It seemed he even knew that I had gone off to find small groups of men to visit with whenever we had nothing scheduled. He thanked me for that.

As soon as I had a chance, I thanked him for sending for me and told him that my experiences in the Philippines had made me more aware of how good it is to be an American, and to be alive.

He seemed to want to talk, and the three of us relaxed. But I was so conscious of all the people waiting to see him that I asked: "Besides all the generals waiting in the lobby, how about all those Japanese waiting in the basement to see you? How come you can take time to visit with us so long on such a historic day as this?"

"Oh, I can't see those men down in the basement," he answered. "You ask that, Ish, because you don't know our enemy as I do. You must understand that the delegation downstairs is here to arrange the details of surrender, and it's made up of a variety of ranks. It is beneath the dignity of a higher rank to negotiate with a lower rank. Captain sees captain, major sees major, general sees general. Since I am Supreme Commander of the United States Forces, I can see only my counterpart, who would be their emperor, Hirohito. If he had come, I would see him. When he does, I will. But Americans would lose face with the Japanese if I confronted any of the others. Those men in the basement are all seeing their counterparts, without their side arms, swords, and knives, which they brought with them on the plane. We took all weapons away from them as they entered the meeting room downstairs. They didn't like that." Then he went on to explain that when they sit down at a conference table, like sits opposite like, and they talk only with their own rank.

General MacArthur asked if there was anything he could do for us. I told him I would like to have an autographed photo, because otherwise no one would ever believe I had really met him. "Oh, I'll be glad to give you one," he said. And he picked up his corncob pipe and lighted it again. He took an eight-by-ten glossy from a drawer and, without asking me how to spell Ish Kabibble, took a whack at it, and his spelling of it turned out atrocious. My name was just a conglomeration of letters. When I saw it, I must have looked crestfallen, because he asked, "What's the matter?"

"Well, two things. I appreciate this very much. I'm sure you know that. But gosh, you misspelled my name, and I wish I could have another picture with my name spelled right. Nobody will believe this says 'Ish Kabibble.' Besides, in this one you only have four stars, and you're a five-star general. I hate to ask, but if I could, I'd love to have a five-star picture."

He laughed. "Well, you *would* notice that!" He tore up the first one and pulled a more recent picture from another drawer, saying, "I don't have many of these left, but I am glad to give you one. Now write down exactly how to spell 'Ish Kabibble.'" I did so, and he copied it and got it right. I thanked him again.

He wanted to know if we had any questions for him. We said that we should leave, since we had been in his office for more than an hour. But he said: "No, don't go. Let's talk. What do you want to talk about?"

When it was my turn, I said: "One thing I've always wondered. You know, we hear a lot about mistakes we made, like Leyte Gulf and so forth—cases where Americans were killed because the Japanese knew we were coming and their intelligence was better than ours. I'm sure that wasn't always true, but I guess what I'm trying to say is if we made so many mistakes, how come we won the war?" In reply he made a very simple statement. What he said was simple, but when he speaks, his voice has such an authoritative ring to it that it sounds almost like the voice of God. "Wars are not won by the side that makes no mistakes," he said. "Wars are won by the side that makes the fewest mistakes, and they made more than we did."

After that, we left for the docks to catch our boat to Cavite. The harbor was littered with sunken Japanese ships. From our boat we could see Bataan and Corregidor.

## The Ways of Peace

> You never know what chocolate ice cream tastes like till you've tried vanilla.
>
> —Anonymous

Not long after our audience with General MacArthur, we had to pack up and move out of the house where we were staying, to make space for thirteen generals who had arrived from Europe to see MacArthur. We left our belongings on the porch to keep a lunch date with Major Graham, who took us to a Chinese jeweler who had hidden jewels of Manila families during the Japanese occupation. He also made jewelry, but it was far too expensive for us.

Then we moved out into the jungle to General Clovis Byers' house, which had not been occupied since the Japanese left. Doors and windows were gone, light bulbs missing, plumbing and wiring ripped out. It was a mess, but at least it was a roof over our heads—except for mine. I drew a room with a bomb hole in the ceiling and spiders as big as toads, toads as big as dogs, and rats almost as big as cats. Jungle vine had grown into the room and out through the bomb hole.

We set up cots and netting. We had no water, no lights, no food, nothing. What a godforsaken place to have to stay. But we were lucky to have a place at all. With all the activities going on in Manila in connection with the peace treaty, it was a scramble to find anywhere in or near the city to get in out of the rain.

We sent for a gas-powered contraption that was supposed to give us electricity, but it did not work. Fortunately, some GIs in the area fixed it for us.

Kay and I were invited to eat at the WAAC headquarters that night, and the girls were invited to eat at the enlisted men's mess hall. The WAACs had made a big chocolate cake, and on it was written in white frosting, "TO KAY AND ISH."

The next morning we got up at 4 A.M. to leave for Okinawa to do our sixteen extra shows in the next eight days. We were told to leave early, because in the afternoon Okinawa "weathers in" and visibility gets poor. We drove to General Eichelberger's for a five o'clock breakfast. When we got there, he was in his bathrobe frying eggs for us. His houseboy had overslept, and the general was anxious that we get an early start. He clowned around and told us stories and jokes while we lolled in chairs and almost fell alseep. As it turned out, we did not leave Manila until after eleven and did not arrive at Okinawa until 4:25 P.M. Our plane had needed repairs.

We were amazed that Okinawa is so large—sixty miles long and ten miles wide. Six hundred Air Transport Command planes were assembled at the airport where we landed, and there were eight or nine other airfields on the island. We were driven to the 233rd General Hospital, where Kay and I bunked. Okinawa is a beautiful island, the Japanese vacation spot. The weather was very cool. But that night I was too tired to sleep, or the problem might have been that the lizards yelled all night long.

Next morning I took a shower under a barrel in the woods. Talk about cold! At 9 A.M. we flew to the other end of the island, where 2,500 Japanese were still fighting. They did not seem to know that the war was over. Our 1st Marine Division was there.

A four-hour jeep ride took us to a camp where we did another show. That night I stayed in a tent belonging to a Colonel

Scott. My cot had *springs,* and he gave me a quart of stateside bourbon.

Once, as I was on my way to the can, General DeWitt Peck called me up to his porch to have a cold beer and talk. From the porch it was a two-hundred-foot drop to the ocean, and we sat looking at the terrific view. We could see Ima Shima and also Ie Shima, where Ernie Pyle died. Japan was just three hundred miles over the horizon. All of a sudden some beautiful music floated to us from behind the house somewhere. I went around to take a look, and there was a sixty-piece marine band set up in the woods. The reason? To serenade the general and his guests. It almost broke me up. The general told me they were stretcher bearers for the 1st Marines, one of the toughest outfits in the war. And here they were, having been dragged out to serenade us! I felt small. I was just a private who, but for the grace of a trumpet and a few jokes, might be sitting in that band having gone through hell myself in the fighting.

I immediately wanted to walk over and talk to the men in the band. I hurried to them and shook a few hands. I felt I had a million words of thanks for each of them, but all I could get out was, "You're all great." Then I had to take off to get ready for the show.

The following night, during our show at a base called Womb Tombs, four Japanese stood on the crest of a hill beside an officers' club, and one of them threw a hand grenade into the audience. After the show, we heard that no one was seriously hurt. We were told that the Japanese came all the time to watch the shows. One Japanese had sent a letter to Special Services complaining about the movies shown. He said that he had attended Hollywood High and that he knew there were better movies. "Get on the ball," he urged.

On our way home that night, we stopped to see General Vinegar Joe Stilwell at his headquarters. He had a wonderful meal spread for us, and real scotch. Twenty minutes before we arrived, he told us, a Japanese soldier had thrown a grenade at his quarters. It had not caused much damage, and the soldier had not gotten away. While we ate, riflemen were posted like flies all around the house. General Stilwell said, "Those riflemen will lie there all night if they have to, until finally that guy will try to get away and we'll grab him."

The next day we flew to Ie Shima. Following the afternoon show, we went to Ernie Pyle's monument, erected at the spot where he had been killed. From there it was about a mile to his grave, which is a simple cross, like those of the GIs he is buried beside. Tears ran down the cheeks of big, strong men.

That night, back on Okinawa, General Griswold, my fellow Erie native, came backstage after the show to say hello. I also met lots of other Erie men on Okinawa and the nearby islands.

Late that night, I stood out in the rain naked and washed the Japanese dishes I had bought. There was no point in standing in the rain with my clothes on. I would have had to put on wet clothes in the morning. And it rained on Okinawa most of the time, day and night.

It was now nearing the end of August, and we had only a few days more on Okinawa. They proved to be memorable ones. When you are about to leave a place that has meant a lot to you, every new person you meet, and every person you have to say good-bye to, seem to take a special hold on you. They represent a rich experience you are leaving behind. We met General Louis Woods, who had funny hats made for Kay and me. He called them "hot pilot caps," and their peak extended about two feet outward from the part that sat on the head. We met Colonel Paul Tibbets, who piloted the plane that dropped the bomb on Hiroshima. We ran into my friend Haig Ouzonion, with whom I had worked for a while at an airplane parts shop in Los Angeles when I was trying to do "my bit" for the war effort and also make a little extra money. Haig was drafted just before I was, and the army had him repairing carburetors. While I was on Okinawa, he did everything he could for me. He got me a foot locker for the items I was taking home. He gave me three cartons of assorted cigarettes and woke me up in the morning if he thought I might oversleep. I gave him the tool kit I had taken off the Japanese Red Cross ship.

On our last Sunday on Okinawa we had nine thousand men in our audience at the afternoon show. I was introduced to General Josef R. Sheetz, who had played a big role in our attack on the island. A colonel took me up through the hills, caves, and destroyed towns. "The battle for Okinawa ended in these hills," he said. "But there are still about a thousand Japanese up here in isolated groups, still holding out. They're cut off from their units and don't know the war's over."

Monday we did the 2 P.M. show in a pouring rain. Afterward, at the mess hall, we found General Jimmy Doolittle waiting for us. What a gracious host he was! And he acted just like a regular guy. I sat at his table, opposite him, and laughed all through the meal at his one-liners about his diminutive size. "I felt like one of the lesser gherkins at the Heinz plant," he said at one point. Another one was: "If all guys like me were laid end to end, they'd reach practically nowhere." In all fairness, I have to say that Jimmy Doolittle had some of the crispier jokes I heard during the war years.

He lent us his own B-29 and crew to fly to Iwo Jima for two shows and then on to Guam. From Guam we would go to San Francisco.

So we were not going back to the Philippines, and I knew now that I would have to go home without having found any sign of Bill Merz. I had told my niece Marian that I would try to find her husband around Manila. I had inquired everywhere but never found him. After the war, we compared notes and learned that at times we had been within thirty miles of each other.

We took off from Okinawa for Iwo Jima early one morning with me in the nose bay. The plane used 180 gallons of gas just to taxi down the runway and get airborne. When we started down the runway, my nose was about two feet off the ground up front. What a feeling! In no time we were doing 120 miles an hour, and at about 130 mph we took off, over the coast and out over the decks of hundreds of boats, all pulling anchor, headed for Japan. We were headed in the opposite direction. I could hardly believe we were going home.

After five hours in the air, we landed at Iwo Jima. The island had not had rain for three weeks, and everything was dry. Runways were cracking, and volcanic steam shooting up through cracks.

We were taken to General Frederick Hopkins' quarters. We swallowed our lunch, did our show, and then drove to Mount Suribachi to see where the marines had planted the famous flag. The 3rd, 4th, and 5th Marine Divisions landed there on

February 19, 1945, and in six days they had taken Mount Suribachi. Then they had to fight another twenty-three days at the other end of the island before it was declared securely under American control. We visited the three marine cemeteries.

We played to mostly navy that night. Just as Kay introduced me and I arrived at the mike, all the lights went out. We walked offstage and had to wait till they were fixed. It was very windy. Later the audience presented the band with eleven bottles of stateside liquor and eleven cartons of cigarettes. Kay made a warm thank-you speech, and I thanked the crowd for the use of the trumpet and also for not complaining about my playing. Since arriving in the Pacific, I had been playing two tunes at each show—"Rockin' Chair" and "Honeysuckle Rose"—and not having my own horn with me, I had had to borrow one for each performance.

Sterling Tracy, who did the radio show "GI Journal" on Iwo Jima, had breakfast with us at General Hopkins' the next morning. He had not been able to see the show, because he had been on duty at the radio station. He wanted us to say hello to his wife at the Crosby office. He cried when we told him we were going home. Everybody wanted to go home right away. That was the hardest time to be overseas. If you were not going home, you felt forsaken.

We landed at Guam in the afternoon. We heard that Trudy Erwin had been through there that morning on her way home. She had been one of Kay's female vocalists after Ginny Simms left. Charlie Ruggles' show was waiting somewhere on the island for transportation home. They told us that no planes would be heading for the States for twenty-four hours. We had to stay overnight, but we were promised the first plane out in the morning. I wanted to wire Janet that I was on my way home. But I was told that the Red Cross cable took several weeks.

We ate with General Tom Harding and went to a movie. Next morning the plane was ready, but we were delayed because the door of the plane would not close. So we helped install a new door. Kay and I wore the "hot pilot caps" that General Woods had made for us back on Okinawa.

Finally we flew off, from Guam to Kwajalein to Johnston Island, each leg approximately an eight-hour trip. We crossed the International Date Line and had two Fridays on the journey home. I kept trying to reach Janet with long-distance telepathy: "Janet, I'm coming! Listen hard, Punkin'. Do you read me?"

We arrived in Hawaii at 5:30 one morning. A lot of red tape held us up there. All our souvenirs had to be closely inspected. We waited and waited for all the official papers to be made out. At one point we went to Waikiki Beach for a dip and then had dinner with Edgar Rice Burroughs, author of the Tarzan books.

At one o'clock Sunday morning we were in the air headed for San Francisco, and at two in the afternoon we saw mountains ahead, which meant we were home. More than twenty enlisted men were in the plane with us, all returning veterans who had been in the Pacific three or four years. As the shoreline grew, there were many reactions. Some men obviously felt uncontrollable joy; others stared, unbelieving; some cried a little; and a few seemed apprehensive, even nervous. I tried to imagine the various situations that these men were coming home to. After so long, conditions would probably be changed drastically for some of them. But for all that, I was sure it was good to be alive. And I wished that everyone who had gone over could be coming back!

# 4

## THE POSTWAR YEARS
## ISH'S ONGOING ADVENTURES

## Rough Going

Worry is stuff that if nobody did it, there'd be nothin' to about.

—Ish

Since the war ended at the same time Kay's tour ended, I was returned to New York and, instead of being reassigned, was discharged in October, 1945, at Fort Dix. My army record says that I won the Asiatic Pacific Ribbon, the Philippine Liberation Ribbon, and one star for Okinawa. Standing about fiftieth in a long, hot discharge line, I heard a voice from far behind me yelling, "Hey, Ish!" I turned, and way back in the line stood Red Skelton, waving happily at me. I waved happily back. We were getting out at the same time.

In December, Kay's radio show, "The Kollege of Musical Knowledge," went on the air in New York under the new sponsorship of the Colgate-Palmolive-Peet Company. At that time Janet and I were living in Beverly Hills. Kay wired me to come to New York. But few of the old gang were available. Harry Babbitt and Lyman Gandee both had jobs they liked in Los Angeles. So the singer who had taken Harry's place when Harry was drafted, shortly after I was, was rehired. His name was Mike Douglas.

Although the show stretched through two more years, it was not on the air during the summers. After our first lean summer, Janet and I determined never to have another one. Suppose we teamed up and went out on the road the following summer with an act of our own? Why not? Janet had a natural theatrical bent. She had taken ballet as a child and was graceful, petite, and attractive.

But we wanted help in putting an act together, and we turned to a person who stood out in my mind as a master comedian and pantomimist—Ben Blue. I was a fan of Ben's from watching him during his days on Melrose Avenue when he worked at Slapsie Maxie's in Hollywood. Then he moved over onto Wilshire Boulevard with Sammy Lewis and Bennie Lessee. Ann McCormack was the girl, and the band was Phil Harris'. Above the bandstand was a stage where they did the "blackouts"—quick scenes with a punch line followed quickly by a blackout.

His most famous sketch—or the one that I remember best—which set me to practically rolling on the floor, was his upper-berth routine. I could never get enough of it. I laughed myself silly every time I saw it. Janet and I had gone to see him often.

So when we wanted someone to write an act for us, we naturally thought of Ben. I called him on the phone and told him what we wanted to do—put together an act for a thirteen-week theaters tour while Kay was on vacation the next summer. Would Ben coach us? Yes, he would do it, he said. "But I charge, you know," he added. "How much?" I asked. He named a pretty good figure. I had to think a minute and finally said, "OK, I'll pay it."

Ben said: "You come to my ranch in the Valley tomorrow, and we'll set up a schedule of three or four afternoons a week. Come about two o'clock, and we'll sit around the pool and I'll write you an act."

The next day when we gave him our check, he immediately made a phone call and bet the entire two thousand dollars on a horse. Janet and I dropped a few inches. We had worked so hard to save that money. But we sat around the pool and had some chitchat, and later Ben turned on the radio, made another phone call, and came back to the pool with the comment, "Well, there goes that." His horse had lost. Our money had come and gone. But if he turned a hair, we did not notice it.

He would start to show us some pantomimes, but we would be laughing so hard at Ben that we had forgotten why we were there. Soon his two little boys showed up on tricycles, circling around the pool and around us, racing each other. Suddenly they rode right through the plate-glass window, smack into the living room, with glass flying in every direction. Ben's only comment was: "They play real nice together, don't they?" He said not a word to them. Occasionally, if they got in his way, he thrust a backward kick at them, yelling "Get lost!" and then he went right on talking to us.

Ben had little wheels built into the soles of his stage shoes. That was the secret of how he skimmed around on the pool tiles explaining pantomime. Every time we went there, we drove away laughing over how funny Ben Blue was without even trying.

In the summer of 1947 Janet and I did our act together, opening at the Hippodrome Theater in Baltimore, for Izzy Rappaport. After our first show, Izzy said, "What are you doing with Ben Blue's material?" (Izzy knew everybody's act.) "He taught it to us," I said. "I paid him two thousand dollars to coach us." Izzy said, "Well, Ben should know better." He went to the phone, called Ben, and said, "Give this kid his two thousand back." And between that first show and our next appearance an hour or so later, Izzy wrote us an act using my material. Ben did give me my money back.

The William Morris Agency of Beverly Hills booked us for thirteen weeks in thirteen cities. We called our act "Effie Lee and Ish Kabibble." The "Effie" came from Janet's mother's name. We toured with the Henry Busse show some of the time.

When the Colgate-Palmolive-Peet radio sponsorship ended in 1947 after two years, Kay broke up his band and went out on his own for the Pillsbury Company, performing alone. Times had changed since before the war. Kay had had the Lucky Strike program for nine years, but now show business was restless. The word *television* was in all the sponsors' minds.

For the first time since I had joined Kay in 1931, I was unemployed. At first I thought: "So what? I'll get something." But then it started to rain—rain bills—and we had not saved a dime for a rainy day.

I took stock. Janet and I could have gone out again as a team, since our act had gone over well. But because the children were in school, we could not take them with us, and hiring someone to stay with them and keep house would have been so expensive that we would have barely broken even.

It seemed to me that other people in similar fixes always had something to fall back on, like a small, lucrative side business or an oil well or someone to borrow from or even a teensy-weensy inheritance. In books set in England, characters always make do on small inheritances.

But I was alone. I did not even have an uncle in show business. No relative had raised me in a trunk backstage. No angel was there to speak for me now. I looked around, and even behind me, but nobody was there. Nobody was looking around to see if I was looking around.

I thought back over all the people who had offered me "big stuff" in recent years. One man offered me a top job as a disc jockey. He said he would make me big. I said no, I was with Kay. I was a Kay Kyser man. David Butler had wanted to put me under contract to him for movies a few years before, but that time Kay said no. He told David that he had me under contract and would not release me.

My trouble was that I had a sense of loyalty to my employer to a fault. I did not protect myself. I never once thought, "Well, Ish, and when are you going to strike out and make *your* million?" Back in 1931 I had said, "The next band I go with, I'll stay with, come what may." But I had not expected "come what may" to arrive before I was forty. Now I had to find work, since my family had a tendency to want to eat.

I did a few "shorts," as they were called. These were popular in the days of crowded movie houses, before television. Bob Benchley used to do them. His included *How to Fold a Card Table* and *How to Go to Sleep.* One of mine was called *How to Learn to Ride a Horse.*

For a few weeks I worked with Jimmy Wakeley's TV show on KTLA in Los Angeles. Then I helped Tex Williams with his TV show from Knott's Berry Farm on Sundays. The pay was very low. I took over Orval Knapp's orchestra after he was killed in an airplane crash, and directed it at a ballroom in Santa Monica. But none of these jobs brought in enough dollars to pay the bills.

In 1948 sales of television sets were beginning to take off. We did not have one yet, but one night we rented one for a dinner we gave for Charlie and Marian Ruggles. It was probably a Tuesday night, when people who did not yet own a set congregated in the living room of a neighbor who did and watched Milton Berle en masse, eating popcorn. It became a way of life. People who lived through the early days of television can never forget those neighbors with whom they watched Milton Berle.

In the 1940s the Bogues were good friends of the Ruggleses, who were two of the most beautiful persons we ever knew. One night just before Christmas one year, they were at our house for dinner. The children were very small. Charlie was growing a beard for a movie role, and about 7:30 he asked, "Could I say good night to the kids?" So he went to their door and peeked in, and though Pete, who was then five or six, knew Charlie, the little girls, with their minds on the season, asked right off, "Are you Santa Claus?" So Charlie played the part, talking like a Santa would, telling them how close Christmas was and to be good little children. It was the highlight of the girls' Christmas that year, and Charlie loved it.

Years later, when Janet and I first moved to Palm Springs, we lived upstairs over a dental laboratory. It was a rather long climb from the street. One day Charlie was in town, but we did not know it. Janet and I went to the store, and when we got back, there was a note on our door at the top of the stairs: "Just dropped by to say hello. Sorry you weren't here. Love, Charlie." Charlie had climbed those stairs, though he should not have, given his heart problem. We were sorry not to see him. As it turned out, that was our last chance, since he died not too long after.

In the late 1940s I once tried to step out of the Ish Kabibble role. It almost worked. Why didn't I try again? I don't know.

My agent sent some pictures of me in regular face and attire to Warner Brothers, and director Mike Curtiz spotted them. "That's the guy I want," Mike said, and he ordered me tested for the part of one of Joan Crawford's boyfriends in *Flamingo Road.*

"Stand down. Sit up. You get the part," said Curtiz. I went unrecognized through wardrobe, make-up, and other tests, and people asked, "Uh, what was your name again?" A couple of actors on the set wondered about where they had seen me before. But I kept quiet. My hair was combed back, and without my "dumb face" they could not place me. I kept quiet.

Then came the big scene with Miss Crawford. "Aha," I thought, "she'll recognize me. We played together in USO camp shows." But she did not recognize me. The script called for me to knock some coins from her hand, which I did with such gusto that I knocked off one of her fingernails. I thought, "Now I've done it!" But she smiled, insisting it was her fault. Then the publicity man for the movie began to tour the cast, and the game was up. I had to confess, "Yes, I'm Ish Kabibble." I combed my hair down and assumed my dumb face, and extras from nearby sets came over to see what the laughter was about. The director was alarmed. "If he's funny in this picture, it will be serious," he said.

The next movie I did was *Ridin' High,* with Bing Crosby at Paramount. Today's television reruns don't give me much footage, what with the cutting they have to do. But the full-length movie showed me singing a whole song face-to-face to Bing. The song was one I have mentioned before—"The Owner Told the Trainer, the Trainer Told the Jockey, the Jockey Told the Horse, and the Horse Told Me." But if you are ever watching *Ridin' High* on TV and miss seeing me because you went to the bathroom or sneezed, you can at least hear me at the end of the movie when the poor horse dies. That's Ish Kabibble playing taps.

Then I got a part in *Young Man with a Horn,* starring Lauren Bacall. During the shooting of that movie, I worked often and got very good money, but I wound up on the cutting-room floor. That's nothing to beef about. Better men than I have ended up there.

In the summer of 1949 we sold our house on Willaman Drive in Beverly Hills and bought another nearby with a clogged sewer that the owner forgot to mention. Lots of money went down that drain. Then came the carpeting and a completely new kitchen. And then came the wire from Kay saying: "COME TO NEW YORK STOP AM REORGANIZING BAND FOR WEEKLY TV SHOW FORD MOTOR COMPANY KOLLEGE OF MUSICAL KNOWLEDGE."

The only personnel back from the old band, besides myself, were Jack Martin, singer and saxophone player; Bill Fontaine, arranger; and Mike Douglas, singer. Carl Hoff was hired to lead the band, since the television format made it impossible for Kay to be both master of ceremonies and director of the band.

Our Thursday night TV show lasted fourteen months, and then the lightning of unemployment struck again. On Christmas Day, 1950, Kay informed the members of the band that he was retiring to North Carolina and we were not to report for rehearsal the next day. Janet and I wished each other a Merry

Christmas and laughed because we didn't want to bawl in front of the kids. Besides, we were not the only ones; the whole band was suddenly out of work.

After the holidays, I hung around the MCA offices in New York, cooling my heels, hoping that someone there would notice me. Before this time, when I was working, people treated me like King Kabibble whenever I went into these offices. But now everyone was looking right over the top of my head.

I was about to give up, since it seemed that about all I was doing by being there was creating a nationwide wave of disinterest. But then I must have gotten in somebody's way, because MCA booked me with Guy Lombardo for several weeks in Hartford, Connecticut, as a stand-up comic. Heretofore comedy had been rather out of Guy's line. I played my trumpet, too, but alone, as part of my act, not with his band.

To be with Guy was a big boost for me, a great personal satisfaction. Guy had never before included a comedian in his band. Many bands did, and it was also popular to have a boy singer and a girl singer. All bands had them, with one exception: Lombardo. "If a man does not keep pace with his companions, perhaps it is because he hears a different drummer. Let him step to the music which he hears," Henry David Thoreau once wrote. He did not have Lombardo in mind, but the passage makes me think of Guy. Surely his success can be attributed to his doing it "his way."

I once asked Guy how the band's style was created or where he got it. He just said that they played that way because it was the best they could do. I mentioned the shimmering tones of his brother Carmen's saxophone. Guy said Carmen played the way he did because it was the only way he knew how to play.

Many bands copied Guy. Bands often copied bands. But it is one thing to copy and give credit, and it is quite another to copy a style and then claim you originated it.

There is one story about copying bands that I would like to clear up. A situation developed concerning Kay's singing song titles that has confused the public for years, and it is my feeling that someone should speak the truth about it. And I am just the one to do it.

In Santa Monica in 1934, Kay and the band, as I have said, spent many hours after work, long into the nights, developing a style of our own in which the singing song titles were very prominent. We took that style to Chicago when we followed Hal Kemp into the Blackhawk Restaurant that year. George T. Simon verifies this in his book *The Big Bands,* and after describing Kay's singing song titles, he sums up their significance: "It was simple, but it immediately attracted much attention. . . . It was a unique and ingenious image-building device."

When George Washington Hill took us from the Blackhawk to New York to do his Lucky Strike radio program, we found that Sammy Kaye was using our style as his own. He was not only claiming it as his but implying openly that Kay had stolen it from him.

The true history of the singing song title, however, follows this chronology: First, our band invented the singing song title in 1934. Then, about six months after we opened in Chicago with it, Sammy Kaye began to copy it from us. At the time, Sammy was playing in Cleveland in a cellar dine-and-dance place on Euclid Avenue called the Log Cabin. According to Ralph Flanagan, who later became famous on his own, Sammy and he would meet, listen to us, and wire-record our arrangements, singing song titles and all. So by the time we got to New York, Sammy was using the technique of the singing song title as his own. Blue Barron was also using it, but he told Kay, "I owe it to you, and I say so." At one time seven or eight hotel bands admitted that they were using our style. But Sammy Kaye went right on claiming the format was his. Unfortunately for us, many believed him, perhaps because he said it so often.

In Guy Lombardo's recent book, *Auld Acquaintance,* he complained in his mild, polite manner about Sammy Kaye's tendency to "hang around and imitate." I think I know what he is talking about. I realize it's all water under the bridge, but I want to set the record straight.

## Mike and Ish

> A farm is a hunk of land on which, if you get up early enough mornings and work late enough nights, you'll make a fortune—if you strike oil on it.
>
> —Fibber McGee

Now and then after Kay retired, Mike Douglas and I would happen to meet or somehow get together, and we usually wound up discussing our shaky job situations. Neither of us had made enough money since the breakup of the band, and we were running scared. Mike had a great voice, and he sang with good expression. He had two little girls—twins—and his wife Genevieve. Later they had another girl. I had three children and Janet. We had to feed all these faces and pay for a roof over their heads.

We decided to put an act together and take it out on the road for a while. If we could get booked, it would be better than nothing. We already had plenty of nothing.

We sketched out our act without the assistance of a writer, since we did not have enough money to hire one. In our act Mike came out first, after we had been introduced, and he started to sing a song. I think that first song was "It's a Great Day." Once he reached the first or second chorus, I peeked around the corner of the wings with my bangs down and, assuming my dumb face, took a step or two out onto the stage. They put a spotlight on me, like they already had on Mike, and I stood there watching Mike sing.

I kept the audience's attention by moving another small step out onto the stage. It was the oldest formula in show business for getting laughs—setting up dignity and then knocking it down. I stood there, seemingly reluctant to come out while he was singing. Then slowly I walked up behind him and tapped him on the shoulder. He stopped singing, turned around, and started to bawl me out for interrupting him: "What's the matter with you? Who are you? What are you doing out here on this stage?" I answered without making any sense, and we had a short conversation with some funny lines.

"Can't you see there's a show going on here? I'm singing a song!" Mike exclaimed.

"Oh, OK. So I'll get off and let you sing your song." Then I left, and Mike sang "The Old Lamplighter" to much applause, toward the end of which I came back onto the stage carrying my horn. "OK," I said, "I let you sing your song. Now you gotta let me do somethin'."

"*You* can play that?" he asked, pointing to my horn.

Then I played two or three songs, such as Clyde McCoy's "Sugar Blues," Henry Busse's "Hot Lips," and Harry James's "Ciri Ciri Bin." I could make these songs sound almost like Clyde, Henry, and Harry, which, of course, was like waving the American flag. Then I sang a silly song, and next Mike and I did a number together, with him singing and me standing behind him playing my trumpet. Then we hit the ending and got off.

Whenever you worked up an act, you had to try it out somewhere in order to get booked. In other words, you had to get booked into a tryout theater in order to get work. Acts such as ours were played in big movie theaters as part of stage shows that were added attractions. The bulk of these theaters were on their way out. Television was coming. There were probably only twenty-five to thirty of these big houses left in the whole country where an act might run for a whole week or sometimes for a split week. But nightclubs were also a possibility. So our first objective was to get booked into some tryout theater where we could be seen and judged by audiences and by a booker.

At that time there was a small break-in theater in Brooklyn that was famous for trying out new acts. The audiences knew that and did not expect to see polished performances. It was there that Mike and I first did our act. Kay and Georgia Carroll, his wife, came to Brooklyn to see us on our first night, and a booker was also watching to size us up. As it turned out, what Mike and I really did during the whole act was play to Kay, trying to impress our old boss. We were extremely aware of his presence and worried about what he would think. But all went well, and we were booked.

One of our first jobs was in a theater in Miami Beach. Janet had gone to California to have an operation, and for the surgeon she would have no other than her beloved Dr. Irving

Ress. She stayed afterward at Charlie and Marian Ruggles' house. So I had the three kids with me, and we all went to Florida. Mike, too, had his family with him.

I could not baby-sit with my kids, but neither could I leave them alone in the hotel. They were ten, seven, and five. Naturally they wanted to spend the whole day around the hotel swimming pool, and naturally I was sure they were all going to drown.

A fellow living at the hotel, a comedian named Johnny Fazio, spent most of the day at the pool. He gave swimming lessons, and at night he put on a comedy water show to entertain the hotel guests. I made arrangements with Johnny and his girlfriend to more or less watch over my kids—to give them hot dogs for lunch, hamburgers for dinner, and a tuck into bed at night.

One evening Johnny and his girl were busy for dinner, so I gave Pete some money and steered them half a block down the street to the Fontainebleau Hotel with orders that Pete tell the maître d' that he was there to take his two sisters to dinner. After the children were seated, Pete studied the French menu in silence, put it down, and ordered hamburgers for three. This nonplussed the waiter, but he recovered enough to inform Pete that they did not serve hamburgers.

"You will have to order something from the menu," he said, and he tried to help by translating items into English and making suggestions. When he was all through and waiting, Pete said, "We'll take hamburgers." Stymied, the waiter conferred with the chef, who fixed something resembling hamburgers, which the kids all ate with enthusiasm. Pete was apparently satisfied; he left the waiter a ten-dollar tip.

Mike and I were booked into Texas: Austin, Dallas, Galveston, and Corpus Christi. Then we played a country club in Pittsburgh, the Erie Centennial, and the Chicago Theater. When we finished the Chicago Theater, we had no place to go next. Our booking agent was based in Chicago, and the only thing he could get us at the moment was Gussie's Kentucky Lounge. It was on South Ashland Avenue in Chicago and was a bit rough. It had once been owned by Al Capone, but he gave it to Gussie

Mavros as a reward for certain favors, renaming it in the process.

Mike and I opened there the night after we finished at the Chicago Theater. We opened for "an indefinite period," which meant "until we get something better." We did three shows a night except for when "the boys"—Al's henchmen—happened to drop in. They would arrive in their black Cadillacs, in groups of four or five, dressed in black fedoras and trench coats. And they always wanted to see the show right away. Even if they arrived just as Mike and I finished our show, Gussie would walk out and yell "Show time!" We would say, "But we just finished!"

"But *the boys* didn't see it!" Gussie said. So, for "the boys," we repeated the same show we had just finished, and the regular customers who had already seen it had to sit there and see it all over again. When it was over, the boys headed for their Cadillacs at the curb. They walked out of the club backwards, facing the roomful of people, with their hands in the pockets of their trench coats. It was a typical hood exit. Once outside, they turned quickly, jumped into their Cadillacs, and roared away.

Mike and I had Cadillacs for a while. He got the idea that if we drove up to a theater in a Cadillac, it would prove we were somebody. In Texas, Mike found a used Cadillac that looked pretty good, and so did I. From then on we drove up to our jobs with our families in our deluxe cars. I am not sure how much it helped.

Soon we came to the conclusion that we were not making enough money, not enough to put any aside, and we needed to save some for the time our children would go to college. So we decided to go our separate ways. Besides, we had one slight problem. At many places where we played, the theater managers, lacking marquee space for both our names, used "Ish Kabibble" alone. Mike would object, but the managers argued that the name Ish Kabibble was known, whereas Mike Douglas was not well known. I did not blame Mike for not liking it, but I had no control over the managers.

Mike went back to his home in Oklahoma, and not long afterward he got a chance to emcee his own show in Cleveland. From there he went on to make history as a talk show host. For our part, Janet and I went to California, where we bought a GI house out in Reseda. I say "out" in Reseda. Reseda may not be out today, but it was way out then. It was a small town in the desert. One reached it via Ventura Boulevard. There was no Ventura Freeway back then.

Before Mike and I broke up, I wanted to get something nice for him for his birthday. Neither Mike nor I had an extra dime, so I wrote him a check for a million dollars, asking if he minded waiting a few days to cash it to give me a chance to make the million and get it deposited. He was touched and said, "OK, and I'll write one for you." And he wrote me a check for one million dollars. We laughed and threw them in the wastebasket. It was funny at the time—back in 1951. It's funnier now that he has made his million.

For three years or more after Mike and I parted, I did single stand-up comedy and played my cornet, filling club dates and theater dates, mostly in the West and Midwest. Once I almost "made it."

I got a call from Bob Hope. He wanted to audition me. Jerry Colonna had left his show, and Bob was looking for a replacement. He suggested we do a few shows together in front of live audiences to see how it went. We did several. The audiences liked them, and Bob liked them, and he said, "OK, Ish, you're hired!" Janet and I called our babysitter and went out that night and celebrated!

But in a couple of days, I got another call from Bob. He said he liked the show very much, and so did everyone else connected with it—except the sponsor, the final decision maker. The sponsor said: "Ish is too identified with Lucky Strike. When the audience hears and sees him, they will think 'Lucky Strike.' They won't think 'Pepsodent.'" Jerry was also having this problem, I was told. He was too well identified with Pepsodent.

Once again a nickel short and five minutes late, Janet and I chalked it up as another brush with fame. It was not anybody's fault, and I finally got over it. But I almost made it that time, didn't I?

By now I was wondering if I really wanted to free-lance in show business. It's great while you're working. But if you're working, you're traveling all the time. Your children have no place to light or take root. They constantly change schools. Many times you have to leave them all home. You live high while you work, and you dig for pennies when you don't.

Once, when I had had no work for a while, I got some—in Fresno at $850 a week. As soon as I took it, I had three other offers for bookings with much more money, one of which was at the Stardust in Vegas at $1,500 a week. But I could not take it, because I had already accepted the Fresno job. It was a maddening situation about which you could do nothing.

---

## My Funny Club

> The test of a real comedian is whether you laugh at him before he opens his mouth.
>
> —George Jean Nathan

Inside my head for many years there has existed a Secret Funny Club. Working in comedy, trying to be funny, I came to feel a kinship with certain comedians who, to me, are or were funny men. The members of my club are the type of comedian I truly laughed at when I was a kid, when I was in the business, and when I see comic acts today. They are the ones who tickle me deep inside. I never told anyone about my club. Now I have an urge to do so, mainly to honor its members.

There are many types of comedians. A lot of people call themselves comedians, and they are or may be. Some of them are the joke-telling type, and yes, many of those are entertaining and I laugh at them. But they are not in my club. The distinguishing feature of the men in my club is that they can be funny, and portray their funny characters, simply through pantomime. It is not necessary to hear them. You look at them, and they are funny just through their gestures and facial expressions. They don't even have to try.

There are only ten members of my club. No one has to agree with my choices—I don't ask that. Some of them are long gone, but I laugh when I remember them. Anyone omitted is omitted because, according to me, he does not belong. He does not have the necessary qualification of being funny without talking or funny without trying.

None of them, of course, know or knew they belong. Not that they would care. No one ever knew about My Funny Club. I have just carried these guys around in my head and chuckled over them.

The ten are Lloyd Hamilton, Ben Turpin, Slim Summerville, Leon Errol, W. C. Fields, Fatty Arbuckle, Ben Blue, Laurel and Hardy (they count as one), George Burns, and Foster Brooks. I knew four of them to some degree and a couple of them very well.

Back in my Bal Tabarin days in San Francisco, I knew Ben Turpin because he often went to the Bal after work just to go to a nightclub. The first night he showed up, we recognized him right away, and a few of us went over to his table to talk with him and have a drink. One night he stayed till we finished at around 2 A.M., and we all went out front to tell him good-night.

Ben could do a somersault from a standing position, landing flat on his back without hurting himself. In movies he did it when someone said something that supposedly shocked him. Instead of throwing up his hands or some such gesture, he would turn one of his flips straight as a stick.

So that night, as we were talking with him out front, I brought the subject up. "I've watched you do those flips, Ben, and I don't see how you do it," I told him. "You must be a fantastic acrobat."

"Well, I'll show you. I'll do it right here."

"On the sidewalk? You'll break your back!"

"No, just watch!" And he flipped, landing flat on his back on the cement, got up, and went right on talking as though nothing had happened.

When Slim Summerville was appearing in San Francisco he went to the Bal Tabarin almost every night after work. During one of these periods, I was getting the flying trapeze act going, and at Christmastime as an added touch we strung Christmas lights up the sides of the trapeze and over the top of my head about two feet, in the form of an inverted U. I thought it might be funny to leave one of the sockets above me empty and, while singing and gesturing on my trapeze high in the air, to point my finger upward and have it look as though my finger got caught in the empty socket with the result that I got a big electrical shock. Well, I went through this rigamarole several times, thinking it would get a laugh. But the audience did not laugh. There was practically no reaction at all.

I often sat at Slim's table when he came. "Why doesn't anybody laugh?" I asked him one night after he had seen me do it.

"You haven't been in this business very long, have you?" he said.

"No. I just started this act. I'm only doing it because Frank Martinelli thought it up, and I'm trying different things to make people laugh. I'm a trumpet player."

"Your problem is you're not a pantomime artist in any sense of the word. You have to remember that timing is everything. The people in the audience—their eyes and thought, as they see any sight gag—are quite a bit behind you. You know what you are going to do, but they don't. You know why they should laugh. But you have to telegraph it to them in such a way that it isn't done too fast. It has to be done slowly, so that they can follow the action. So you start your finger up there very slowly and let it hover right below the empty socket so that the people will think, 'My gosh, if he puts his finger in that hole, he'll get a shock.' They have to see it coming! Then go on and put it in, and then you can pull it out real fast. You've already delivered the message to them, and they can see that you got the shock. They'll laugh."

At the next show, I did it exactly as Slim said, and I got a big laugh. I will always be grateful to him for that lesson on the importance of timing in comedy.

I met W. C. Fields in the CBS studios in Hollywood at Sunset and Vine during the war. We were doing Armed Forces Radio transcriptions, which were radio programs put together to be shipped overseas to the soldiers in war zones.

Mr. Fields and I were to do one together, and we were seated at a table; each of us had a script. It was a simple thing. We were just supposed to read the script for the sound man. We rehearsed it for a few minutes first. At that time Fields was near the end of his career. He was somewhat feeble, and his glasses did not focus just right. He would read some of the script and become impatient with it and stray from it, delivering a gag or improvising something else that was not on the printed page to cover for the fact that he could not see the words.

Then they would stop us, and we would have to start all over. Soon they had a man stand next to us with a pencil to keep Mr. Fields from losing his place. Of course, that irritated him even more. But we tried again and again, and he kept lapsing into passages that were not in the script, which meant that there was no place for me to answer him. He would tell about the day he took the terrible drink of water, or go into some other famous routine, because the ham would come out and automatically he would give us something he *knew* was entertaining.

So there I sat. We finally got a program made, but I had very little to do with it because he never led me into my lines. It turned out to be essentially a monologue that he ad-libbed. Toward the end he just threw the script away, and still I sat there, though Mr. Fields hardly seemed to realize it. Yet the whole thing was very amusing to me, and we were all grateful to be that close to this legendary, zany character, watching him do his thing. Once we were finished, they had to put the scissors to it and delete some choice bits here and there, but it turned out to be a good program for the boys overseas, though there was very little of Ish Kabibble in the final product. But at least I had a chance to *try* to do something with W. C. Fields.

I have already said what a great fan of Ben Blue's I am. Not long after Janet and I returned from our thirteen-week cross-country tour featuring the comedy act Ben had gotten us started on, he called and asked me to stop by his house. He said he had a project for me.

By now he had moved into an apartment in Beverly Hills. His wife Axie was there, and so were his boys. I think Axie's mother also lived with them. Ben told me that he had "quite a few" eight-by-ten glossy pictures of himself from movies and he wanted them framed. I had mentioned to him somewhere along the line that in my garage, as a little hobby, I had a woodworking shop and often made my own picture frames. He wanted to know if I would make frames for his pictures—simple frames with glass in them.

"Sure, I'll do them for you," I said. He offered to pay me, but I said, "No, no, I'll do them as a favor, Ben." At first I did not think much about the cost of the wood and the glass, but before long I noticed how much I was putting out. I kept thinking each bunch of frames would be the last, and I did not want to ask Ben for money after I had made my friendly offer. But to Ben, money was such an unimportant item that it never dawned on him that his project might be a strain on my wallet. If he thought about it at all, he probably assumed that I grew the wood in my garage.

So I framed and I framed. I would take the framed photos over to Ben's, a dozen or two at a time, and we would find places on his walls to hang them. When I finished them all, there were two things I could hardly believe. One was that I was through, and the other was that there were about two hundred pictures of Ben Blue on the walls of his apartment, and not a single picture of anyone else in the place!

About this time Ben was working up a piece of pantomime in which he portrayed a French artist painting a picture. He had heard there was a man in Hollywood who was going to movie stars' homes to paint portraits of their wives. The artist's name escapes me, but his fee was rather stiff. Ben did not worry about that. He decided to have the artist paint Axie. It would be a big oil painting to hang over the fireplace, and while the artist was painting it, Ben would study the man's movements to apply them to his pantomime. The man looked like a true French artist. He even had a little curled-up moustache. He seemed so typical that any casting director would have taken one look at him and cast him as a French artist. I was in on some of the sittings, and Ben would point out to me how the artist was working. "Now watch!" he said. "See how he holds up his thumb?" Ben would be memorizing every move the painter made.

When the portrait was done—it was quite good—Ben said, "Now, Ish, I want you to frame it." I did not say anything, but I thought, "Well now, this is getting a little out of my league." The canvas was forty inches by thirty inches. I went to a framing studio and got the owner's advice. He said the portrait would require a big, heavy frame and told me where to get the raw molding. So I built and painted the huge frame, which must have weighed fifty pounds, and then Ben and I hung the painting over his mantelpiece. That was the end of our frame relationship.

I was saddened when I heard of Ben's death a few years ago. I saw him last in 1974 when he came to Honolulu, where I was in real estate. He was thinking of buying a nightclub for himself in Honolulu. He had sold his club in Santa Monica, which had done so well for him that he kept putting his profits into adjacent lots on both sides of him until he owned an entire block. Finally, he sold it all for a good price, so he did not lack for dollars in his last years. He was one of a kind, and from the first time I ever saw him perform, he belonged to my private club of great natural funny men.

On the day I saw him in Honolulu, we had lunch together and sat talking for a long time. As it turned out, he decided not to buy in Hawaii. He had had no idea how expensive land and buildings were there. The next day I drove him to the airport to catch his plane back to the mainland. That was the last time I saw Ben.

It is not strange that, as well as I knew Ben, I never told him about my Funny Club, because that was my plan for it. No one was to know. But now it gives me pleasure to remember my club and to call Ben my friend.

## Nichols and Kabibble

To lose a friend is to die a little.

—Honoré de Balzac

In 1955 I formed my own six-piece Dixieland band—the Shy Guys. After a break-in week at Jackson Hole, Wyoming, we traveled the country over. Between 1955 and 1960, if you name the place, we played it: Toronto to Chicago to New Orleans to the Nugget in Carson City to Las Vegas to Harrah's in Reno to Harrah's in Tahoe to Fresno to Denver to various college campuses. Periodically we wound up back in Vegas at the Showboat Lounge, the Stardust Hotel, the Golden Nugget, or the Fremont Hotel. Once we were at the Fremont for a year.

My three children finished high school, went to college, and often worked summers somewhere near wherever I was booked. Pete enlisted in the marines. Time was spinning fast.

In December, 1958, I received word that Dad had died. When I got the phone call, I cried like a baby. But I could not get home; I had to work. We were playing Harrah's Club in Tahoe.

But the month after that, the band played Chicago, and I had a day off. It was a Sunday, and it happened to be my birthday, January 19. That Saturday night after work I got in the car and drove all night, about five hundred miles, to Erie. On Sunday I drove to Dad's grave and sort of talked to him for a while. I told him why I had not been at the funeral and how much I thought of him. That night I drove all night again, back to Chicago, and went to work Monday at noon. I had gone without sleep for two nights, but I felt close to Dad. To me he was the greatest man I would ever know.

Two years before that, I had had a letter from him that I have always liked. It is dated November 9, 1956. He was eighty-four then and had just returned from his annual hunting trip into the Allegheny Mountains. He wrote:

> There is nothing new to write about except I finished my hunting trip and got home safe. There were four men with me. They were good company. We got up at 4:30 and were in the woods at daylight and hunted till dark. It was cold; just a crust of bread in our coattails. We did not see each other all day long—we each hunted alone. I did not see a buck at all, but just wait till next fall. One night I met two of my buddies in the woods and one had a small fawn. It was going to die up there so we brought it in to camp and I fed it an apple and was it hungry! Then we took it to Clarendon to the Game Warden. About 25 hunters came to camp to see the fawn. I hunted four days all day long and felt good when I got in at night by the fire. We had lots of fun. We'd eat early and go to bed. No evening at all down there. Do you know somehow without any reason I have quit smoking. And do you know anyone can stop any habit in case he really wants to. But I am no better off than when I smoked but just as well off. So never to smoke again, unless my "tirt shale" catches fire.
>
> Love,
> Boop

Boop was his nickname, given to him by a small granddaughter, and he used it to order lumber and to write notes to traffic police not to ticket Boop's car.

He hunted deer every year, and in his younger days it had been bear. He never got lost in the woods and, so he said, never used a compass. Once I took him to a store in Ridgewood, New Jersey, to buy him a compass, but he would have none of it. He told the store owner how to roam any woods and never get lost. He said all you had to do was remember where you left your car. He told how to do it. No one in the store understood what he was talking about. But he never got lost. At least, if he ever did, he got found. Being my dad, he probably found himself.

When I was young, as I explained, I bought Red Nichols' records and played along with them to learn hot choruses. I did not know that many other musicians did the same thing. Since then I have read in several places that musicians often learned to improvise dance music by listening and imitating, finally reaching the point that they could phrase right along with the musician on the record.

If I had ever dreamed that by organizing my own Dixieland band I would one day get to know Red Nichols, I would have organized one years before I did. The Shy Guys—my guys—played all around Vegas and throughout Nevada, so we kept running into Red, who would be playing somewhere nearby. Whenever I found myself in his neighborhood, I went to listen to him.

When I first joined Kay, Red often played in the Golden Pheasant in Cleveland, where Janet and I had our wedding reception. Whenever Kay was booked back to the Golden Pheasant, I always tried to get into town early if Red Nichols had preceded us there. That way I could listen to Red for a couple of evenings. Of course, he did not know me then. In those days I had no friendship with him. I just admired him very much.

When I first went into Nevada with the Shy Guys and we were booked into Harrah's Club in Reno, I found that the music in the casinos went almost twenty-four hours a day. The groups in the afternoons were not well-known, but they filled up the time and drew people in so that they gambled. Then about seven or eight in the evening another, better-known group—semi-well-known—came in to play. But the featured groups came on during the prime hours, from midnight to six o'clock in the morning when the big crowds were there. And my band was one of those.

No band can play continuously for six hours, so the custom was that the club booked two name bands for the midnight-to-six spot. They would alternate. One would start at midnight and play forty-five minutes; then the other band would play forty-five minutes. Each band made four appearances in the six hours.

On one occasion that we played Harrah's, I knew ahead of time that we had been hired for the twelve-to-six spot, but I did not know until I got to Reno that we were to alternate with Red Nichols and His Five Pennies! Red's Dixieland music was extraordinary. Nobody in the business played Dixieland like he did.

Dixieland, as music buffs know, is improvised, that is, extemporaneous. Nothing is written down. The musicians just do it out of their heads, ad-lib. And Red did not have anything written down, but his music always came across as so well rehearsed, so well thought out. It sounded like an arrangement that was written down, but it was not. He rehearsed and rehearsed those guys, until they were note perfect.

During our intermissions, I sat out front listening to Red. When we followed him on, it was a great thrill for me to play on the same stage where he had stood a few minutes before.

While we were both there at Harrah's, we had an interesting exchange that was very exciting for me. In my youth in Erie, when I was learning to play by copying Red's sounds, one of his records I bought and worked on so long was "Plenty Off Center"—just to get the feel of his phrasing. This recording of Red's was a musicianly thing with several movements. Each movement started with a melody and then varied. Maybe Red would play one chorus or thirty bars, then break out into a completely different melody, and then come back to the original. And there would be variations on these two themes. "Plenty Off Center" was a masterpiece, and I memorized it. I played it with the Gallagher band and the Presque Isle Six in Erie. In fact, I liked it and played it so much that I knew it like my face in a mirror. Then there came a gap of about thirty years during which I never played it at all. The whole time I was with Kay—twenty years—I never played it.

At Harrah's before the evening started, we often hung around our dressing rooms. Red's dressing room was next to mine, and now that we were playing on the same stage, we were back and forth visiting, though I cannot claim that he was a fan of mine. Red was all music. He did not go in for comedy; there were no comedians in his band. So our music was the basis of our relationship.

One night I wandered into his dressing room with my horn and asked him if he remembered an old song he had recorded called "Plenty Off Center." "No, I don't remember that. It must have been a long time ago," he said. "It was," I replied. And I told him how I had learned to play hot choruses by playing along with his records. I mentioned some of the recordings, and he became very interested. Yes, he could remember some, but not "Plenty Off Center."

I could hardly believe it. "But Red, it was such a great recording," I said. "I'm surprised you don't remember it."

"Well, you know how it was then, Ish. You'd run and record, run and record, and many of them weren't big hits. Maybe some old record collectors would have it."

"I'll play it for you right now." As I said, I hadn't played it in thirty years. But I felt like I could do it, and I picked up my horn and played the song all the way through exactly the way he had done it years before. I expected him to say, "Oh, yeah, I remember it now!" But he didn't. What he said was: "You know, I recognize my phrasing. It's amazing to me that you can play it all the way through, after all these years. And you do make it sound like me." I took that as a great compliment. He went on to say that it showed what a tiny impression some tunes make on some people and what a big impression the same tunes can make on others, depending on the circumstances. He wondered if there was some reason why he had blocked that tune out of his head.

Years later, when I was out of show business and into real estate near Palm Springs, Janet and I, for the first time in our lives, went to Las Vegas for a vacation. It was the first time we had ever been there when I was not working, the first time we could relax in Vegas and not feel in a hurry. We were there strictly to relax and to enjoy the place as customers. We had deliberately picked a time when Red was in town, playing at the Mint. I was greatly anticipating seeing him.

We had been in Vegas for one day when we heard that he had died. We were stunned. He had played only the night before. But it was true. It was a great shock and seemed unreal.

We were staying at the Desert Inn out on the Strip. That evening, restless, I grabbed a cab and went downtown. I wanted to go to the Mint. That very night we had planned to go see Red.

For a while I walked the streets, still stunned. From habit my feet walked into the Fremont, into the Carnival Lounge, where I used to work. I said hello to people I knew around the place. Then I walked half a block to the Mint. Inside, the signs were still up: "RED NICHOLS AND HIS FIVE PENNIES."

I went into the room where Red had played the night before. Red's bandstand was empty; the whole room was empty. But I sat in there for an hour and thought about Red and all my experiences with him. I thought of how I had cut my teeth on the hot choruses on his old Perfect records. Perfect was, like Columbia, a brand name, which seems appropriate, since his music was perfect. I thought of how when Kay's band followed Red into the Golden Pheasant in Cleveland, Janet and I would try to get there for Red's "closing night." From the band's point of view, there are two big nights in any engagement—opening night and closing night. I thought about a time that my Shy Guys followed Red into Marineland in southern California, catching his closing night there. I recalled an occasion during the war when Kay's band played a shipyard near San Francisco. Red had given up his band temporarily—some of his Pennies had been drafted—and I had heard that he was working in that shipyard. I looked him up, and there he was in his steel helmet, working for the war effort. We had a good talk.

And I remembered, like it was yesterday, the time the Shy Guys were alternating with Red at Reno. Red and his band often just stacked their instruments behind the curtain, since they were going to need them again in another forty-five minutes. Sometimes my band did the same, so there were often a whole bunch of instruments stacked back there. One night I picked up Red's cornet instead of mine and did not know it. We had identical horns. But as soon as I started to play, I could tell that I was out of tune. It was half a step flat, so I reached down and pulled the tuning slide in, which raised it a halftone so I would be in tune. The instant I did it, I realized what had happened. I had Red's horn, not mine.

Red lipped his notes up, as it is called. He did not blow a true note straight through the horn. He had to tune it flat because he played everything up a half step higher than was normal. He did it with his lip, forcing the notes up. It was a habit he had, simply the way he played. So, for me, his horn was a halftone flat.

I sat in the lounge in the Mint and relived these experiences, and my memories were so sharp that I seemed to feel Red's presence in the room, and I wanted to say something to him. I wanted to say: "I hope you find a good band wherever you are, Red. You sure left your mark on the world and on me, and I thank you for it."

---

## Orange Coats and Nightmares

> Dreaming permits each and every one of us to be quietly and safely insane every night of our lives.
>
> —Dr. William Dement

I was working in a club in Eugene, Oregon, as a single again, having given up the band mostly to be free from financial concerns about the other five guys. I met a man from Seattle who was a developer of recreational properties. He told me that Ginny Simms and her husband, Don Eastvold, former lieutenant governor of Washington State, were at Ocean Shores, Washington, handling resort property. Since I was in the neighborhood, I flew over to see them.

They were running their own resort area with convention facilities. There was a Ginny Simms Restaurant and a Ginny Simms Motel. The whole setup seemed very attractive to me. The idea of staying in one place was beginning to appeal to me. But I had a lot of club work booked ahead: Vegas, Tahoe, Carson City, even back at the Bal Tabarin. So it was not until toward the end of 1960 that I returned to Ocean Shores and talked again with Ginny and Don.

The upshot of that visit was that by February, 1961, I had my real estate license, and Don, Ginny, and I moved from Ocean Shores, Washington, to a development called North Shore Beach Estates at the north end of Salton Sea, to sell property. I was there with Ginny and Don for four years, and eventually became the company's sales manager and broker, often moving in the summers to other resort areas in cooler states, such as Minnesota and Wisconsin. I got a license in each state we worked. I owe a lot to Ginny and Don for helping me get my start in real estate, and to their sales manager, Cal Hendrick, for teaching me the difference between a salesman and a "closer."

In 1965 I moved to Desert Hot Springs. I sold property for other companies besides the Eastvolds', and at one time I lived in a house next door to former president Eisenhower. I also worked at Clear Lake, above San Francisco, for a year, and then went back to the Palm Desert area, where I sold property for a great guy, Moksha Smith.

Janet and I loved the desert. And I liked selling real estate. In a sense, selling real estate is much the same as being in show business. Instead of talking to a large audience, I talk to a man and his wife. The applause happens when they write the check, and if they do not write the check, it means I did a lousy show.

One day in Palm Springs I ran into George Duning, Kay's arranger, and we sat down to talk things over. "I'm glad to see you, Ish," he said, "because there's something I've been wanting to talk to you about. I want to tell you about these nightmares I've had ever since we were with Kay. I have them quite often."

I stared at him. Then I said: "Now wait, George . . . OK, you tell me yours, and then I'll tell you mine."

He looked surprised and started to talk. But the whole time it seemed I was listening to mine. I began to have exhausting nightmares not long after Kay broke up the band. They involved terrifying experiences from which there was no escape. I would be caught in a web of anxiety and wake up in a cold sweat. It was essentially the same dream, over and over. The details were not exactly the same, but they were always similar.

Bands in the 1930s and 1940s took tremendous care about their dress and grooming. All the big bands were extremely clothes-conscious; their members dressed immaculately. Their suits were tailor-made, and each night they presented a symphony in some one color onstage.

In my early days with Kay, we all wore regular black tuxedos that we had brought from home—some with narrow lapels, some with wide. We could not afford more. But as soon as we could afford it, we got tailor-made suits that all looked alike and were a spiffy color. It happened in San Francisco. McIntosh's was the place to go, and all of us went down and got fitted, beaming with satisfaction.

Kay was a stern taskmaster about our appearance. We were required to have clean shirts every night, polished shoes, and proper uniform. We soon became affluent enough to have two or three different jackets. In the summer we wore seersucker and in the winter another material. Kay always insisted on two things: absolute punctuality and a smart appearance.

Those two rules formed the basis for the nightmares that George and I had. On innumerable occasions over the years, on our way to work we had asked ourselves frantically, "Do I have on the right uniform?" and "Am I going to make it there on time?" If one does this for twenty years, it leaves its mark.

When we were on the Lucky Strike program in New York, we went to the very best tailors and bought several jackets of different colors. We got bright orange coats that we later wore in some of our movies. Those orange coats looked so great that they were our favorites. But we also had French blue coats, red coats, navy coats, gold coats, and coats of other colors. In Hollywood our tailor was Sy Devore.

In the summer we wore white tuxedos, especially when we worked at the Waldorf Hotel or the Pennsylvania Roof. The hotel would furnish a room with heavy metal clothes racks on which forty or fifty jackets could be hung. Right after work we changed our clothes and left our band jackets in the hotel. Driving home in our uniforms would wrinkle the backs, and Kay insisted on perfection in dress. We had to have our jackets cleaned every few days.

Every couple of weeks or so for many years I have dreamed, for example, that I am on my way to work. For some reason—a flat tire perhaps—I am an hour late, and so I am frantic. I arrive at the door of the dance hall, and looking in, I see the band playing inside. I try to go through the turnstile, but the doorman will not let me in. He asks, "Where's your ticket?" I say: "I don't have a ticket. I'm in the band." He says: "How can you be a member of the band? You're not even dressed right. They all have on orange coats. Yours is blue." I try to buy a ticket, but I have no money in my pocket. Then I hear the band come to the place where I am supposed to stand up and do an eight-bar solo. Kay is looking all around for me. My chair is empty. I struggle with the doorman to get inside, but to no avail. I wake up in a cold sweat.

George's nightmares, which were quite similar to mine, were built around not being able to get a song written on time or not even starting it, or being late for some important appointment or rehearsal. After both of us had talked about our nightmares, we sat there staring at each other, unbelieving. We became so interested in the similar patterns in them that we got in touch with other members of the band who were with Kay a long time, such as Lyman Gandee and Harry Babbitt. To our amazement we found that they, too, have recurring nightmares with the same themes. It seemed weird, but on reflection it was understandable.

Recently I had one that is slightly different, in that the mode of transportation is updated. In this dream I am on my way to work; I know I'll have the right coat, since it is at the hotel, and I am on time. But then I say to myself: "The hell with it. I'm not going to work tonight. I'm going to a movie." What has happened to my car I don't know—dreams often do not explain such things. Anyway, I grab a taxi, and when I get to the movie, I am seized by fear and tell myself: "I can't do this. I have to go to work. And I better hurry or I'll be late." I grab another cab, but it turns out to be a skateboard, and the same cab driver I had before is on the skateboard with me. He asks, "Where to?" and I say, "Back to the dance hall!" Taking the skateboard makes me so late that I know the dance will be over by the time we get there, so I decide to go back to the hotel where Janet and I are staying. But I cannot remember the name of the hotel or where it is. After you have stayed in so many hotels over a period of many years, their names cease to register. Often the names are the same or similar, and sometimes you think you're still staying in the place you stayed the night before. So there I am, running up a huge bill on the skateboard meter, skating up one street and down another in a strange town, never once spotting a familiar place or face. I realize that I don't have enough money to pay the cabbie, and I wonder if he will have me arrested. Frantic, I woke up exhausted, relieved that none of it was true.

Is it too much to ask to grow out of this sort of thing? Or should I just "Get used to it/Get used to it"?

---

## Around the World

> If I had to go around the world on my own money, I couldn't get out of sight.
>
> —Ish

In the late 1960s I went to Australia to plan and set up selling procedures for Pat Boone's Ocean Shores development on the ocean at Brunswick Heads. I was alone on this job. I was to design stationery, hire salesmen, arrange for contracts, and handle everything else. There were eight thousand acres to sell, sales were to be made to Australians only, and it all had to be according to Australian law. The property was along seven miles of beautiful ocean-front land with clean white beaches.

In the United States, you think nothing of asking occasionally that something be done or delivered in a rush. In Australia, you rush nobody. They say, "We'll have it in a fortnight" or whatever. They pronounce it "fortnit." A fortnight can be anywhere from two weeks to two months. Whenever they get it ready is when you get it. Once you learn that the hurry-scurry of the States does not get you anywhere over there, you settle down and are nice and get along much better.

Australians are impressive people. They are people of their word, and a handshake means a commitment, just like in Texas. All my dealings there were with Australians, so I got to know them well, and I thoroughly enjoyed them. In fact, I liked almost everything about the place.

I say I liked *almost* everything. In Australia there are many snakes, including three kinds I hated. One is a little brown snake about three feet long and very poisonous. A second is a black poisonous snake something like a rattler. The third is called a carpet snake, because it has many colors, like a beautiful carpet. Its usual length is from twenty-seven to thirty-five feet, and it swallows animals such as dogs, cats, and rats whole. I am not sure why I was so afraid of them. Perhaps it was just because they are so big. At least they are fairly docile. If you happen to step on a carpet snake in the tall grass, it hardly even turns around to look at you.

Some people caught them and sold them to farmers for five dollars each. The farmer would put them in his barn, up in the rafters, and so long as there were rats and mice for the snake to catch, the snake stayed up there, maybe for years. There was no reason for it to come down. Every time I went into a barn, the first thing I did was look up into the rafters to be sure there was no carpet snake over my head. But I did not go into many barns. I finally got somewhat accustomed to watching for snakes both on the ground and overhead, but I was always uneasy about them.

The most fun Janet and I had in Australia, I think, was in looking for a place to live. Once we were off the plane and through customs at Brisbane, the first thing we did was rent a car and drive ninety miles south to the project. I am sure it's old hat to people who go abroad all the time. But I had had no chance to practice, and everything in the car seemed to be in the wrong place—the rearview mirror, the pedals, the shift, the hand brake. It was also hard to learn to drive on the left-hand side of the road. In trying not to hit someone, I would swerve in the same direction the other fellow swerved. Finally, we checked into a hotel for two days, so that I could get over the initial fear of driving the car.

We stayed for a time at the Sands Motor Inn, in the heart of the Gold Coast at Surfers Paradise, which is where the tourists go. It was like living in luxury in Miami Beach. But it was expensive, so we had to find a more reasonable place to live permanently. Each day we drove at least seventy or eighty miles south to hunt for a house.

First we tried going to what was called an estate agent. He took us to the little village of Mullumbimby but found he had nothing to show us there. So he sent us to Murwillumbah to see the lady at the post office, who had a flat to rent in Billy-nugel, which is a short distance south of Tweeds Head. She showed us the flat, but after looking at all the rooms, I asked, "OK, where is it?" Janet giggled.

"Where's what?"

"The bathroom."

"Oh, that. That's out in the backyard where it belongs. I wouldn't have one of them filthy things inside my house!"

In *Mrs. Miniver* Jan Struther wrote, "Marriage is having an eye to catch." That is certainly one of the things it is. Janet caught mine, and I caught hers, and we thanked the lady and left.

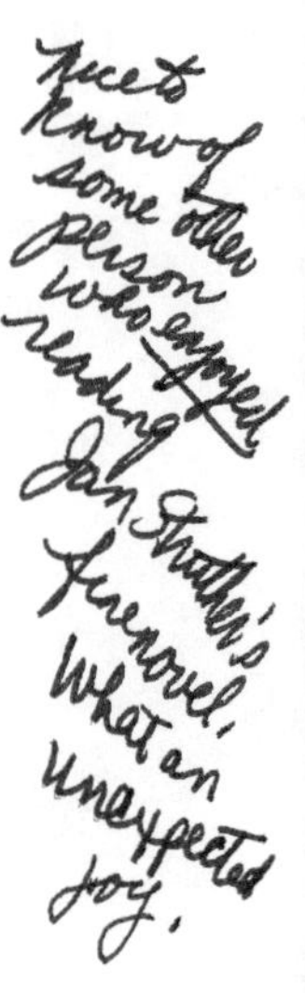


The next day we drove the streets of Bungawalbin, Bonalbo, and Old Bonalbo. Still we had no luck. All of the flats had that same little shack out back. My company engineer suggested Woodenbon, Tunbulgum, and Wollangarra, but the fog set in early that day, and we could not find them. We did run into a gem of a cattle hamlet named Woolloomooloo, which had a tiny railroad station with red roses climbing up and down its ventilator pipe. On the way home, we passed through Gib-beragee, Ballandean, and Broome's Head and had supper in Woolgoolga. The scones there were worth the whole trip to Australia.

All the potential lodgings we had looked at thus far cost from five to seven dollars a week. The rates were always by the week, and the places were furnished but had no baths. Next day we found another estate agent and told him we had to have an inside bath and shower. "Well, I know of one place," he said. "But I don't think you'll want it."

"Why not?"

"It's so expensive!"

"How much?"

"It's nineteen dollars a week!"

The townspeople snubbed us for a while, calling us pluto-crats for paying nineteen dollars a week for a place to live. But they soon got over it.

One day I saw the same agent unloading bricks on a vacant lot in downtown Brunswick Heads. I asked him what they were for.

"I'm going to build a two-story building with four apart-ments—one for me and my wife, one for the grandparents, one for my son and his wife, and the other one to rent," he said.

"You've already rented it. I'll take it," I told him.

"But I'm going to have to ask twenty-five dollars a week for it furnished."

We watched the building go up, and when it was finished, Janet and I moved in and remained there until we left Australia. It had everything—a washer and dryer, an inside bath and shower, and a hand-painted toilet lid. Hand-painted toilet lids are a big thing in Australia. At least they were back in 1969 and 1970. The whole time we were there, I never saw a john that did not have a hand-painted rose or some pretty, flowery design on its lid.

Nearly every day brought an Australian surprise. We learned that the women have a custom of visiting one another at ten in the morning, in hats and gloves, for tea and cakes and conversation. And reciprocation was definitely expected. For Janet that was something of a shock, since it was entirely possible that at ten in the morning she might still be in the hay.

But we became fond of Australians. We sat on our porch and watched them gather in the park across the street from our new place. People there do things with their children; teenagers are part of the family. In the park was what they called a "housey tent," where all sorts of family activities go on—bingo, picnics, wood-chopping contests. Whole families would compete and have a wonderful time together.

We had been told before we took the Australian job that we could have a month off at some point and return to the States for a vacation. When the time arrived, we decided to travel through Asia and Europe. We knew it would be a whirlwind trip, with little time for prolonged sightseeing, but at least it would take us around the world.

Our trip had many highlights, of course, and not a few adventures. In Manila we found no reminders of my wartime experiences there with Kay. But we saw only the airport. We were shocked, after our long flight from Sydney on a plane with "no conveniences," to find huge rats under the airport benches and both rest rooms closed for repairs. So we had to endure till we landed in Hong Kong a couple of hours later. The highlight there was the ferryboat ride at night across what is often called Fragrant Habor between Kowloon and Hong Kong proper.

In Tokyo, where Janet and I had been earlier on a brief vacation, we visited a famous temple in which conveyor belts under the floor carry the coins offered by worshipers to the counting room. I had one of Tokyo's famous baths, but all I got out of it was all wet and a cold.

In Bangkok we went to TIM Land (the TIM stands for Thailand in Miniature), where there are displays of Thailand's exports and crafts and an amusement park. We watched Thais working on textiles and with silkworms. There was also a pit containing innumerable cobras, and a volunteer from the audience was taught to defend himself against the deadly hooded cobra. The keeper asked the audience to pick out a snake—to assure the crowd that the cobra was not defanged or coached ahead of time—and in a special area, the keeper taught the volunteer to stand perfectly still while the snake reared its head and swayed, watching its potential victim. But as long as the man did not move, he was safe. I could not watch and walked out. Janet stayed for the whole performance, watching the man sweat.

In New Delhi we passed up the Taj Mahal when we learned it was a 120-mile bus ride away. So we drank martinis and mailed postcards of the Taj Majal. We sent an unsigned card to Lyman Gandee, reading, "I knew a Gandhi once." The taxi drivers in New Delhi tear to the airport at eighty-five miles an hour. I am a forty-mile-an-hour man myself.

As we landed on the runway in Beirut, the plane crew made us pull down our window shades. But I peeked. The runway was lined with soldiers with machine guns. We soon found out that a plane had been blown up the day before. In Istanbul we did not get to see much. The Hilton was fenced in to keep merchants off the grounds. I tried to take a walk outside but was so pestered by the street vendors it was not worth the effort. We wanted to see the dancing brown bears, but we were disappointed.

Then it was on to Frankfort, where I tried out my college German by attempting to order drinks in the hotel bar. After I had stumbled through it as best I could, the bartender said, "OK, Mac, whaddya want?" He was from Brooklyn. In Rome we went into St. Peter's where the pope was expected. A big crowd began to pour in. The rush of humanity trying to squeeze in scared us; besides, we had a cab waiting outside. We pushed and fought against the incoming mob and finally made it out before the pope arrived. It was the first time we ever walked out on a pope—and probably the last. In Paris we stayed at the Hilton at the foot of the Eiffel Tower. We saw the famous paintings in the Louvre, and also some broad in clay with no arms. I became so interested in Leonardo da Vinci that I decided to buy a book on his life. I called a nearby bookstore to reserve one and took a cab over to pick it up. The clerk said it was fifteen dollars. It was a beautiful book, all done up in cellophane and never opened. I bought it but did not open it until we were back to Australia. At last I removed the cellophane and opened the book, and it was all in French! And I cannot read French. Stupid, eh? But I am Ish Kabibble, and I always say that what I lack in ignorance I make up for in stupidity. Naturally, when you buy a book in France, you should know what language it is likely to be in.

Next stop was London, where we saw Big Ben, Number 10 Downing Street, and the changing of the guard. As everyone knows, they have an exceptional marching band. In New York we saw my sister Gladys and her husband Bill Reilly. Next we flew across the country to Seattle to visit our son Pete and his wife Diane. In Los Angeles we saw our two daughters, Pam and young Janet and their families. Then we flew to Hawaii, where we stayed overnight, on our way back to Sydney and home. So we had been around the world.

I brought home hats from all the countries we visited, which brings the number of hats in my collection to around 130. Sometimes I don one, put on an appropriate face, and peek around a hall corner to amuse a visiting relative or friend.

While in New York, I went to an electronic store somewhere in the 50s to buy a good walkie-talkie to take back to Australia. I wanted to be able to talk with my salesmen out in the field without chasing after them. The man who showed me the walkie-talkie got to talking with me and another customer about this and that, and I decided to have a little fun. I watched for a chance to say to the salesman: "Well, that's because you know your business. You know the electronic business—I can tell that."

After saying it, I went into a little routine I used to do onstage when I was with Kay: "No matter how much you get to know about *one* thing, there's always somethin' else you're not as good at as, 'cause if you *was,* you wouldn't be as good at the thing you are at *now,* 'cause if you're gonna be as good at *two* things as you are at *one,* the chances are it's gonna be the very thing you're not as good at as you are the other, if you are, and if not, nearly every time?"

The two men looked at each other, not knowing what to say. Finally the clerk exclaimed: "Say! There used to be a guy on radio or TV who said something like that. I can't think of his name—it was a crazy name. You must remember him. He had bangs and used to recite goofy poetry and played the trumpet."

"Did he have bangs like this?" And I made my hand flat and pulled it across my forehead just above my eyes, with an Ish Kabibbleish flourish.

"Yeah, that was him. His name was Isky . . . Iska . . . Ish . . . Ish Kadribble, I think."

The customer came alive. "You mean Ish Kabibble," he said.

"That's it!"

"Oh, yeah, I kind of remember," I said. "But I've been in Australia and out of touch."

"But that guy was killed about a year ago," the clerk said.

I snapped to attention. "*Who?* This Ish Kabibble guy?"

"Yeah. A big Mack truck hit him. Killed him instantly."

"Is that right?" I asked. It was not hard for me to look surprised.

"Sure. It was in all the papers."

I picked up my walkie-talkie, which I had already paid for, and said: "That's a shame. I hadn't heard. But as I said, I've been in Australia, out of touch. I wouldn't know. Well, thanks a lot." And I walked out of the place.

Why should I have tried to convince this man? He knew all about me. Who was I to argue with him? It would have been his word against mine. And it was no new thing. It has happened a lot. Ish Kabibble? "He's dead, you know." Many other show people experience it, too. Or else people just don't believe me.

For a while I worked for two San Diego gentlemen, Art Leitch, then president of the National Association of Realtors, and his partner, Bert Fields. In two years Bert taught me more about how to buy and sell real estate than I had learned in my previous twenty-five years in business. Bert used to call me up from San Diego or fly over to see me on Maui. But he could not believe that I was Ish Kabibble—or would not believe it. "What do you want to latch on to a name like that for?" he would ask. "What would the real Ish Kabibble be doing selling real estate on the remote island of Maui?" He always called me "Riko." He would call me up from San Diego, asking for Riko. I asked him where he got that name. He said he had read a book by Jack Douglas, who wrote about Ish Kabibble, but Bert was sure I was not Ish. It got to be pretty funny to me.

How easy it is to be wrong! We learn how even when we are little kids. Our young Janet was running a day-care center at Palm Desert a few years ago. She taught her two- to four-year-olds to sing "Mairzy Doats" because her father used to sing it. The end of it goes, "A kiddle e divey too, wouldn't you." One little three-year-old always sang, "Ivy'll kill a kid too, wouldn't you." And she *knew* it was right!

## Go! Go! Go!

I've been very busy lately
Goin' lickety-split here
Lickety-split there
Lickety-split here
Lickety-split there.
Going to have to quit it—
I split my lickety.

—Ish

After I finished in Australia, I accepted an offer to work in Houston. It was a welcome change, since we would be able to see our children more often. They were building families and making us grandparents.

After I had been in Houston a month or so, I received a phone call from Merv Griffin's manager, who asked me if I would go to Hollywood to appear on Merv's two-night television special that was to feature band leaders and personalities from the Big Band Days. About a dozen were available to appear: Freddy Martin, Bob Crosby, Stan Kenton, Vaughn Monroe, Les Brown, Lawrence Welk, Horace Heidt, Connie Haines, Helen Forrest, Johnny Long, Charlie Barnet, and Xavier Cugat. And there was also Ish Kabibble, who looked forward to such a reunion.

While waiting my turn to go on, I looked around the Green Room, where everyone sat watching the monitor, waiting to be called. I caught sight of myself in the mirror. Suddenly I saw that my face had been wrinkled by the desert sun and winds. I had been away from show business a long time. But we all looked over the hill.

When Perry Lafferty walked into the Green Room and came over to me, I could have bawled. He put his arms around me, saying: "When I heard you were here, Ish, I had to come down to see you. I even left my dinner." He had to know how happy it made me to see him. Back in our radio days Perry had been the director of our shows and a good friend. Now he was up on the top rung—vice-president of CBS-TV in charge of programming in Hollywood. I was as pleased as a kid with a high-flying kite.

A month or so later there was another such program, and I got a call from Merv's manager again. But this time I was tied up with my job and could not make it.

During the taping of the first special, I had offers from two of the band leaders to join their bands. "Ish—I need someone like you," both of them said. But I no longer wanted to live in a suitcase.

Later in the year I accepted an offer to go to Hawaii to sell property on the island of Kauai for Daniel K. Ludwig. The main office, managed by Jack Bennington, was in Honolulu. So we moved there, and Janet and I bought a fabulous condominium apartment—a penthouse—in a high-rise called the Regency-at-Kahala. We could see ocean from any window. It was the first time in our lives that we could afford a deluxe-view apartment to match our "His" and "Hers" binoculars.

There was a little restaurant in Honolulu behind our office building, up an alley, and it was called the Swiss House. It was run then by a short Jewish Italian who had a Japanese cook who made the greatest Swedish pancakes with fresh strawberries and syrup, with Polish sausages, and if you topped it off with one of his French pastries, it was a bit of all right. I went there about once a week, usually alone, and had my noon jollies.

Altogether we were in Honolulu three and a half years, and

at the end of that time the property on various islands that Ludwig's company had bought up for resale was all sold. The company returned to the mainland.

One week Janet and I wanted to stay in Hawaii for the rest of our lives; the next week we would feel homesick for "the good old U.S. of A.," as Archie Bunker called it. Jimmy Durante used to sing a song that included the question: "Did you ever get the feeling you wanted to go / And yet you had a feeling you wanted to stay?"

Living in Hawaii is an interesting experience. What I find so amazing now is that we fought the Japanese in World War II, that we ever had such a great hatred for them. We were taught that we are better than they are. And here we are now, living among them, and it is clear that we are not better at all. On the Islands we are all the same. We deal with one another, whatever our roots, every day of the week. We get along with one another, we go to parties with one another, and we are fond of one another. The war is over; for some it is forgotten. Then why was there all that killing? Why all those bitter feelings? If the heads of state of all the various countries involved had not provoked the war, those lives could have been saved. Why does mankind do it? For money, fame, or power? But wars are not permanent. You get over them. Take the one between the North and the South; we got over it. I don't mean to stand on a soapbox, but there I was, living side by side with the Japanese we fought—and I liked them! We are still fighting today in other parts of the world. It is as if humanity has not learned a thing over all these centuries.

Our question now was whether to stay in Honolulu or go back to the mainland. My company had gone back. Across the nation, real estate sales were in a slump except in one or two spots—Houston, for example. Houston was booming. The man I had worked for there urged, "Come back if you can." Janet's sister Frances lived there. The song goes, "If I were a rich man . . ." If I had not had to work for a living, perhaps Janet and I would have stayed in Honolulu for the rest of our lives. And in Hawaii people come to you. All your friends and relatives love to visit Hawaii.

So we moved back to Houston, but before we got unpacked, two things happened. First, one of my relatives sent us a clipping from *Midnight,* one of those weekly news tabloids. There was photo of me and a long story with an astounding headline spread all the way across the page: "WILL ROGERS HELPED ISH KABIBBLE BECOME A MILLIONAIRE." Gladys had attached a note to the clipping: "Why didn't you tell us?"

Janet and I were surprised. We were rich? We knew nothing at all about it. The gist of the story was that Will Rogers had told Ish Kabibble that the way to make a million dollars was to buy up large pieces of property midway between two large cities and wait for the cities to grow closer together, when, lo, the price of the property would skyrocket. This, the story went on, Ish Kabibble had done, and he was now a millionaire.

It made mighty interesting reading. But it was not true. In my whole life, I never once met Will Rogers, never even saw him except in movies. Somebody had concocted the story!

The second thing that happened before we unpacked in Houston was that I received a phone call from Ed Woodland asking could I fly to Hawaii immediately to sell some condominiums on Maui. I had a reputation among many West Coast and Hawaiian developers as "the best real estate closer in the business," which never hurt me any.

"What do you mean 'immediately'?" I asked Ed. He said, "Like tomorrow?" I said no to that. But in less than a week we were on a plane. "Here today, gone to Maui," as they say.

To live on Maui and be paid for it was a dream come true. But there we were near Lahaina, and I sold condominiums by the bushel and the peck. They were furnished condos on the ocean, beautiful and expensive. When the right people came to look, I was able to sell them. Janet and I soon bought one.

The complex had several shops, a beauty salon, and a grocery alongside. There was also a nice restaurant, done in Hawaiian decor, with piano bar and cocktail bar. Next door was my office, which was done in white rattan furniture. Even my typewriter was white. I also had lots of Hawaiian plants.

In the evenings we sat on our lanai—which would be called a porch in Erie—gazing out over the blue Pacific toward Molokai and watching the magnificent sunsets. But on some nights

Janet and I yearned for our California desert. On other nights we got out our "His" and "Hers" binoculars and watched the migrating whales play leapfrog with the porpoises.

There are two sides to Maui—"this side" (the one you are on at the moment) and "da udda side" (the other one, as expressed in Pidgin English). If we went to shop on "da udda side," while we were there, it became "this side" and we lived on "da udda side."

When we first went to Lahaina, I inquired around town for a good barber. Several people recommended the Agena shop. Patricia Agena was more than a barber. A haircut by her was a thoroughly enjoyable, indeed never-to-be-forgotten experience. Pat was born on Maui, of Japanese parents, and has never left. Her shop, which is built on the front of her home is clean, light, and air-conditioned. It is located in downtown Lahaina on a quiet, narrow street bordered with so many lush Hawaiian flowers and plants that one felt as if he could almost float through her front door on the aroma.

"Aloha, Mr. Kabibble, come in!" she would say. "I have your confidential haircut waiting for you." Pat and I called my haircuts confidential, because when she finished with me, nobody could tell I had had one but the two of us. When I stepped into her shop, she had my favorite Alfred Apaka Hawaiian music playing. Once the cutting was over, she did a fantastic Japanese-style manipulation of my neck and shoulder muscles, which was apt to put you to sleep if you did not watch out. Then I paid the modest bill.

But the best part was yet to come: a lazy walk through the lush Hawaiian flower garden in her backyard. It was so quiet, and so private, though Mr. Agena would be there sitting almost buried in the colorful mass of blooms. "Aloha, Mr. Kabibble!" he said. "The weeds grow faster that I can keep up with. How are you this afternoon?" I would reply: "Fine, Mr. Agena. Your flowers are especially beautiful today."

All my show business life, my haircuts were very important to me, and I always had to coach the barbers. There could be no sleeping in the chair for me. I had to explain that I made my living with my bangs, and I would comb them down to my eyebrows and say: "Now don't cut any of this except to even the line. And then just cut a little at the back and around the ears." But I had to watch each barber, or he would start cutting the way he wanted to. A fast-cutting barber could put me out of business. My bangs were my trademark, and they were made up of my very own hair, not a wig.

One day in New York, as I was leaving a Lexington Avenue barbershop where I had just had a haircut, I wondered: "What would happen if I went right now to, say, five barbershops and asked for a haircut? Would the barbers take my money and pretend to give me a cut? Or would they say, 'Mister, I don't think you need one'?"

I decided that I wanted to find out. It seemed that it might be an interesting way to pass a free couple of hours. Each time I explained about the bangs, and then sat back and waited. Sure enough, they all took my money, but the last three did not cut much hair. They rattled their snips around my head, picked at strands of hair, and, in disgust, murmured something like: "Ugh, dirty hair. I suggest a shampoo." After four or five shampoos in a row I had just about had it. I bet I had the cleanest head in all of Gothamtown that day. But I don't blame the barbers. Their business is cutting hair, and in every case I walked in and "asked for it." And I love New York and always will.

## Maui No Ka Oi

Roses are red,
Violets are purple,
Sugar is sweet,
And so is maple surple.

—Ish

There is a saying that is popular all through the Islands: "Maui no ka oi" (Maui is the best). I have a love affair going with Maui. The reason is quite simple: to me it is one of the last peaceful yet civilized places I know of in the whole world.

In 1981 Janet and I returned to Houston and lived there for about a year, trying to forget Hawaii. But then we hopped a 747 jet and headed for our beloved island "home." We have traveled all our adult lives and lived in many places, but there is only one Maui.

Maui has beautiful wet green mountains that are often framed by immense rainbows. Some of them are double rainbows, like the one we saw our first morning back and rushed to grab a camera to snap pictures of. The island is perfumed by trade winds that scatter the delicate fragrance of tropical blooms everywhere. My love affair with the place began soon after we first arrived there. As with most such relationships, there was a special day when it became serious. I was with our company attorney, and we had intended to fly to Hana, where Lindbergh is buried. When he knew his end was near, he said, "If I have to die, I would rather live one day on Maui than a year in a New York hospital." So he was flown to Hana on a stretcher and lived there for over a year. He is buried in a grave that an elderly native Hawaiian helped him to dig in the old Hawaiian way.

By mistake, instead of flying to Hana, we got off the plane in Kahalui and drove the rest of the way in a rented car—a pink-striped jeep. The trip was fifty-three miles on a narrow road with ruts, sharp curves, and drop-offs hundreds of feet above the sea. But what I saw during the three-hour journey was worth every bounce. Rainbows fell beside golden waterfalls, and peaceful pools mirrored shower trees, blue skies, plumeria, and orchids. The pools held the reflection of moss- and vine-covered mountains whose peaks were lost in crowns of clouds. Had Dorothy Lamour climbed dripping wet from one of the pools, I would not have blinked. Someday I am going to make that drive again.

I also enjoyed driving into Haleakala Crater, which is big enough to hold all of Manhattan. Another of my favorite things to do is relax on the steps of the old Pioneer Inn at Lahaina, with a Harper's and water (no ice) in my hand, watching the sun go down over the sea behind Lanai and Molokai. Lahaina was once the capital of Hawaii. Later, around 1850, it became a whaling center. The town is old and weatherbeaten and lived in—the sort of place one visualizes when one thinks of the tropics. Outside the Pioneer Inn expensive yachts bob beside the dock, and inside the Whaler's Grog Shoppe tourists sip a drink called the Harpoon (one slug and you're hooked).

North of Lahaina the sea washes against three of the best beaches I know of anywhere—Kaanapali, Kapalua (where we now live), and Wailea. Beside country lanes in Kapalua in rural Maui, Hawaiians still grow taro, raise pigs, and make poi by the sea. Down the road a piece from us on Napili Bay is the Restaurant of the Maui Moon, where a meal is a great experience.

One night I had dinner there to watch the sunset, and I talked with a Hawaiian boy named Nelson Waikiki, who is known as Hawaii's ukulele virtuoso. Someone had tried to persuade him to leave Hawaii for a career on the mainland. "You could earn a fortune," he was told. Nelson smiled, shook his head, and said, "But why should I leave, when everything I want is here on Maui?" If I have my way, I often tell myself, my moving days are over, because everything *I* want is right here on Maui.

Yet sometimes I cannot help but ask: If all we want is here, why do we spend so much money phoning Seattle, Denver, the Palm Desert, Houston? Why do we need to talk to all those places? Are we getting island happy again? Here we can only go to "da udda side." Do we really want to live in one place for the rest of our lives?

We never really unpacked everything after our last move. Perhaps the ideal state would be freedom to wander, to go where we want whenever we want.

---

## The Living End

Memories are forever;
Dwell only on the best.
—Ish

I was sitting about five feet from Bix Beiderbecke in the bleachers of an outdoor stadium in Uniontown, Pennsylvania, listening to a Paul Whiteman concert and watching Bix's every move. Bix was sitting with the brass section at the top of the bleachers along with Andy Sechrist. Nearby were some of the other greats I worshiped—Frank Trumbauer on alto sax, for instance. And who could forget Goldie on trumpet, Jack Satterfield on piano, Mike Pingatore on banjo?

Bix was aware that I was watching him, so he probably knew that I was a fan of his, though he had never seen me before. After playing a particularly great eight or sixteen bars that was exclusively Bix, he would sit down, lean back, and glance nonchalantly over at me as if to say, "How did you like *that*?" My smile was my answer. It said, "Fantastic!"

I had driven to Uniontown by myself from Morgantown, West Virginia, where I was attending college. I had a decrepit thirty-dollar Ford. No one else had wanted to come, but I would not have missed it if I had had to walk. Just a few years before, while learning to play my trumpet, I had tried to copy Bix's playing. But no one could ever really copy Bix Beiderbecke. He had a velvety quality in his tones that could not be duplicated.

Bix had an extra-long straw inserted into a Coke bottle he kept in the inside of his uniform jacket. He drew on this straw, and then, out of his coat pocket, he would get a handful of peanuts and chew on those.

I never met Bix, but that didn't matter. To me he was a legend even then. It was enough for me just to be there that night. It was a night I will never forget.

We were in Hollywood. The band was doing a picture with John Barrymore. He was playing the role of the Great John Barrymore in his declining years—playing himself, in other words. At one point he was to do the soliloquy from *Hamlet* with tears in his eyes.

The prop man was standing by with the glycerin bottle to drop the fake tears on his cheeks. But Barrymore did not need them. At this time he genuinely was in his declining years, and he knew it. The entire crew and all the actors also knew it. A hush came over the sound stage as the camera moved in close and he began, "To be, or not to be, that is the question . . ." The tears came without help. They also came to the eyes of the entire group, who realized that this might be the last time he would ever perform this scene. As it turned out, it was, for he died shortly after the completion of the movie.

During the shooting, groups of us would sit out on the lawn of the huge mansion where the filming was taking place. It was a costume picture, but there was no such thing as air conditioning, and we were all hot. We would sit under shade trees, and on more than one occasion I found myself sitting and talking with Barrymore alone and hanging on every word of the stories about his escapades that he was telling me.

And then there were those memorable jam sessions. Back in the 1930s and 1940s, whenever a band played a town for any length of time—a week or two, a month, or more—word would go out periodically: "There's a jam session tonight." Most clubs closed around one or two o'clock in the morning, and six or eight or ten guys—anyone who wanted to—would meet after work at whatever club was available, and jam the whole night, until six or so in the morning. Wives and sweethearts and friends—anyone who wanted to come—sat around and listened.

We would play and play, improvising Dixieland or whatever, until we might have collapsed. But we never thought of quitting, because we never knew we were tired. I would not have missed one of those nights. They were the most fun of all.

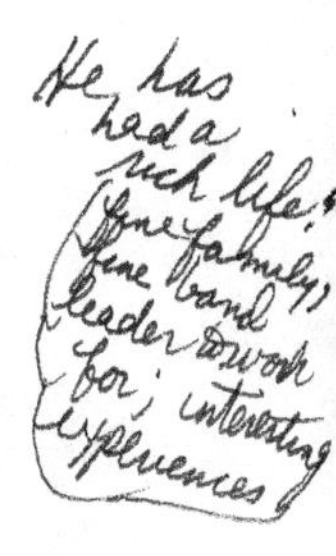

"Awkward is funny," Ben Blue once explained to me. It's not always easy, he said, to look awkward. But if you are right-handed, then use your *left* hand to tip your hat, carry the cane, smoke the cigar, or open the door. Whatever you do in the scene, he said, do it with the wrong hand, and automatically it will appear funny. It works! It was one of Charlie Chaplin's secrets.

Back when I was still in school and before I joined Kay Kyser, I went out on the road one summer with Mark Goff and His Club Miami Orchestra. For some reason, we got stranded in Bluefield, West Virginia, where Mark broke up the band.

That sort of thing happened all the time. When it did, you just bought a copy of *Billboard* or *Variety* and looked for a job in the classified ads. Small band leaders in outlying cities often advertised for players. The sax player and I found an ad reading "Needed: Cornet and saxophone players for summer. Salary open. Call me collect. Ange Lorenzo, Petoskey, Michigan." We phoned the number the ad gave, and we got the job. But we were broke, and so we asked Mr. Lorenzo if he would advance us railroad fare. By Western Union he sent us railroad fare plus an extra ten dollars to eat on.

We played all summer at a drugstore called Julerette's, in a little dance hall on the side of it for wealthy summer vacationers from Chicago who owned big mansions there on the lake. Our theme song was "Sleepy Time Gal." It had just become popular, and Ange Lorenzo had written it. Out front he advertised, "ANGE LORENZO AND HIS TUNESTERS—WRITER OF 'SLEEPY TIME GAL.'"

About twenty-five years later I was selling real estate, and we were living in Palm Desert. Very late one night, while listening to radio, I heard a fantastic recording of "Sleepy Time Gal" that featured a trombone solo that was so great that the tone was like syrup coming out of a pitcher. I was so affected by it that I called the station and was told, "That was Murray MacEachern on that trombone." I asked how I could reach him and found out that he lived in Redlands.

The next day I called Murray, told him I was a fan of his, and told him who I am. He said: "Oh, yeah, I've heard of you. I worked with Jack Martin. He used to be with your band." We had a nice conversation, and he invited us to a little café and dance hall that he owned in Redlands. "Come on over, and bring your horn and your wife," he said. But we had been all through that, many times, at Nick's in the Village and everywhere else. We just could not do it anymore.

So I never got to meet Murray. But I have great admiration for him. I did ask him: "How come you can play that great? Where did you learn to play trombone with all that feeling?" And he said: "My teacher was a great inspiration to me. He was always telling me, 'Never pick up your instrument unless you have something to say.' I never forgot that."

When I look back across my life to the Big Band Days and think of other musicians who had something to say, who played from the heart, I think especially of Red Nichols and Bix Beiderbecke on cornet, Benny Goodman and Hutch Hutchenrider on clarinet, Earl Hines on piano, Joe Venuti on violin, and Tony Motola on electric guitar. Oh, how they could play!

Being a part of the Big Band Era was great. It seldom felt like work. I had fun almost every day, and though I don't claim to have set the world on its ear, people listened and laughed, and I will always love them for it.

"Was it hard to do?" one of the Seven Dwarfs wanted to know.

"Oh, no! It was very easy!" answered Snow White, full of good cheer.

In I come,
Down I sot,
I wrote a book,
And up I got.

Ish Kabibble died on Sunday June 5, 1994.

Mom heard the sad news on KCTC Radio at 7:20 A.M. on June 5th.

He was 86 years old.

September 12 2000 is the day that finished reading this wonderful book. This is the third time that this writer has read this gift. As I may be moving from this gracious old Victorian within a year, this reading is the last time in THIS home. The book travels on with me!

# Index

**kay kyser, 79 — july 23, 1985**

Kay Kyser, who presided over the popular radio program of the 30s and 40s, *Kay Kyser's Kollege of Musical Knowledge*, headed a highly rated band during the swing era which had many successful recordings. During the war the band toured about 500 camps, bases and hospitals on the

Classic Images Sept 1985

USO circuit. One of his biggest hits was "Praise
The Lord and Pass The Ammunition." Kyser had
be... active as a Christian Scientist after he retir-
e...

In T...
Some ... film appearances were in *My Fa-
vorite* ...*ates*, *Carolina Blues*, *You'll
Find Out*, ...*he World*, and *To Be Or Not
To Be.*

Kay Kyser

Kay Kyser and his Orchestra appeared in these fun movies: (* = I saw the film)

* 1. That's Right, You're Wrong (1939)
* 2. You'll Find Out (1940)
* 3. Playmates (1941)
* 4. Around The World (1942)
* 5. My Favorite Spy (1942)
* 6. Stage Door Canteen (1943)
* 7. Swing Fever (1943) see p116 of Ish Kabibble's autobiography
* 8. Thousands Cheer (1945)
9. Carolina Blues (19??) 1944 see page 116 of Ish Kabibble's autobiography

On August 20, 2000 Harry Babbitt was the Featured Performer on Chuck Cecil's Swinging Years. Chuck Cecil has interviewed Mr. B. three times: in 1973, in 1982, and in 1987.

2022 note, written on May 20th Today on THE WALTONS METV (from 12:00 NOON-1:00 P.M.) Kay Kyser was mentioned by one of the characters in THE WALTON family in Season # Seven, Episode # 23 from 1979. This episode is set in the Spring of 1942.